THE SIGNERS

THE SIGNERS

The 56 Stories Behind the Declaration of Independence

DENNIS BRINDELL FRADIN

ILLUSTRATIONS BY
MICHAEL MCCURDY

Walker & Company
NEW YORK

First published in the United States of America in 2002 by Walker Publishing Company, Inc.

Published simultaneously in Canada by Fitzhenry and Whiteside, Markham, Ontario L3R 4T8

For information about permission to reproduce selections from this book, write to Permissions, Walker & Company, 435 Hudson Street, New York, New York 10014

Library of Congress Cataloging-in-Publication Data

Fradin, Dennis B.
The signers : the 56 stories behind the Declaration of Independence / Dennis Brindell Fradin ; illustrations by Michael McCurdy.
p. cm.
Summary: Profiles each of the fifty-six men who signed the Declaration of Independence, giving historical information about the colonies they represented. Includes the text of the Declaration and its history.
Includes bibliographical references [p.] and index.
ISBN 0-8027-8849-1—ISBN 0-8027-8850-5 (reinforced)
1. United States. Declaration of Independence—Signers—Biography—Juvenile literature. 2. Statesmen—United States—Biography. 3. United States—History—Revolution, 1775–1783—Biography. [1. United States. Declaration of Independence—Signers. 2. Statesmen. 3. United States—History—Revolution, 1775–1783.] I. McCurdy, Michael, ill. II. Title.
E221 .F83 2002
973.3'13'0922—dc21
[B] 2002066364

The illustrations for this book were created on scratchboard.
Book design by Claire Counihan

Visit Walker & Company's Web site at www.walkerbooks.com

Printed in the United States of America

2 4 6 8 10 9 7 5 3

Contents

INTRODUCTION

Americans celebrate Independence Day each July 4 because of a document that was adopted on July 4, 1776.

This paper, which announced that the thirteen colonies had separated from England and become the United States of America, has been called the nation's birth certificate. Upon hearing about it, George Washington said that he hoped the document would inspire his troops to win the war for independence against England. The paper's stirring words, "We hold these truths to be self-evident, that all men are created equal," have inspired Americans in war and in peace for nearly two and a half centuries.

This document, of course, is the Declaration of Independence.

Its roots go back to the 1760s and early 1770s, when England taxed the thirteen colonies on tea and other items. In 1774 American leaders gathered in Philadelphia at what was called the First Continental Congress to discuss their grievances. The troubles grew worse; in April 1775 war between the thirteen colonies and England erupted at Lexington and Concord in Massachusetts. A month later, American leaders met again in Philadelphia.

When the Second Continental Congress opened in Philadelphia in May 1775, most Americans still hoped that peace would soon be made and that the thirteen colonies would return to British rule. But the war escalated, and by the spring of 1776 growing numbers of Americans were considering independence. By then it had become clear that taxes weren't the only issue. Having lived for generations three thousand miles from England, Americans had begun to feel like a separate people.

On June 7, 1776, Richard Henry Lee, a delegate from Virginia, arose in Congress and read a proposal:

> Resolved, That these United Colonies are, and of right ought to be, free and independent States; that they are absolved from all allegiance to the British Crown; and that all political connection between them and the State of Great Britain is, and ought to be, totally dissolved.

Many of the delegates were thunderstruck by Lee's proposal. They had discussed separating from England in private, but hearing the words "independent states" formally presented in Congress was startling. Besides, *declaring* independence would be the easy part. Actually *winning* it from the world's most powerful country might be close to impossible.

Wanting a few weeks to ponder Richard Henry Lee's independence proposal, the congressmen delayed the vote on it until early July. Should the vote come out for separation from England, they realized, they would need a paper explaining their action. A five-man committee composed of John Adams of Massachusetts, Benjamin Franklin of Pennsylvania, Robert R. Livingston of New York, Roger Sherman of Connecticut, and Thomas Jefferson of Virginia was asked to produce a paper explaining why America was declaring independence. The committee entrusted the writing to Jefferson.

The tall, redheaded Virginian wrote the Declaration in about two weeks in his Philadelphia lodgings. Jefferson showed the paper to Franklin and Adams, who made a few changes. For example, Franklin improved Jefferson's phrase "We hold these truths to be sacred and undeniable" to "We hold these truths to be self-evident."

The Declaration would only be needed if the independence measure passed. Each colony had formed a wartime government that had sent delegates to Congress. If a colony had five delegates in Congress, three had to vote for independence for that colony to choose separation from England. Seven colonies out of thirteen—a majority—had to vote for independence for the proposal to be approved.

Thomas Jefferson estimated that as of June 1776 six colonies were not yet ready for independence. If just one pro-independence colony changed its vote, the measure would be defeated. But the men who favored independence knew that having seven or even twelve colonies vote for separation from England wouldn't be good enough, for how could a new nation survive with one or more colonies still loyal to England? Unless the vote was unanimous, the colonies could wind up fighting each other.

On July 1—the day before the official vote—Congress debated the issue and took a trial vote. The results showed movement toward independence, with nine colonies now favoring the measure. South Carolina and Pennsylvania were opposed. Delaware was stuck in a tie, with one delegate for independence, one against, and its third delegate, independence man Caesar Rodney, eighty miles away in Delaware. New York's delegates had been instructed by their leaders back home not to vote one way or the other on independence.

An amazing series of events occurred over the next twenty-four hours. Informed by a messenger that he was desperately needed in Philadelphia, Caesar Rodney mounted his horse and headed to the city. Meanwhile, Samuel Adams of Massachusetts and a few other independence men convinced some delegates who were undecided or opposed that all the colonies must stand together.

When the official vote was made late on July 2, everything fell into place. Two Pennsylvanians who opposed independence, John Dickinson and Robert Morris, abstained from voting. This allowed Pennsylvania to squeak by for independence with the slimmest of margins—three votes to two. Wet and exhausted from his all-night ride, Caesar Rodney arrived just in time to swing Delaware's vote to independence. Not wanting theirs to be the only colony against the measure, the South Carolinians switched to independence. And although its delegates did not vote on July 2, New York made the independence vote unanimous several days later.

The July 2 vote transformed the American colonies into the United States of America. The delegates expected that July 2 would be honored as the new nation's birthday. John Adams wrote his wife, Abigail, that he believed Americans would celebrate each July 2 "as the great anniversary festival. It ought to be solemnized with pomp and parade, with shows, games, sports, bells, bonfires, from one end of this continent to the other, from this time forward for evermore."

But what happened was that, after making more changes, Congress adopted the Declaration of Independence on July 4, 1776. Copies of the Declaration were sent to the thirteen states, as the former colonies were now known. American patriots loved the Declaration. And because at the top of the document it said that the Declaration had been approved on July 4, 1776, Americans began thinking of July 4 instead of July 2 as the nation's birthday. This misconception about the day the United States was born has continued to the present time.

Another widespread misconception is that all the congressmen signed the Declaration on July 4, 1776. Most historians think that only John Hancock and Charles Thomson, the president and secretary of Congress, signed that day. It appears that the full Congress didn't sign a copy of the document until later. Most of the delegates signed this copy on August 2, 1776, and others signed even later. On January 18, 1777, Mary Katherine Goddard, editor and publisher of the *Maryland Journal and Baltimore Advertiser*, became the first person to publish the full Declaration, including all the signers' names.

The fact that the Declaration was approved on July 4 but not signed by most members of Congress until about a month later meant that those who voted for independence were not the identical group of men who signed the document. About a quarter of the fifty-six signers had not been in Congress at the time of the vote. For example, Richard Henry Lee was called back to Virginia in mid-June of 1776. As a result, Lee missed the vote for his own independence proposal, but he returned to Congress in late August and signed the Declaration.

The signers of the Declaration, rather than those who voted for independence, have long been honored as the nation's founders. That is because, by placing their names on the Declaration, they announced to the world their willingness to risk everything for the cause of independence.

The British targeted the fifty-six signers for special punishment. The homes of twelve signers were burned, and nearly twenty of them lost much of what they owned. According to some estimates, nine signers died as a result of hardships they suffered during the Revolution. Yet not one signer changed his stance on independence. All of them kept the promise they had made in the Declaration of Independence—that they would stake their "Lives . . . Fortunes, and . . . Sacred Honor" on their country's cause.

Note: The exact order in which the Declaration was signed is not known. The order in which the signers are presented in this book reflects both the history of the Revolution and the signers' relationships to one another. For example, Massachusetts is presented first because it was the site of major events leading to the Revolution; within the Virginia chapter, George Wythe precedes Thomas Jefferson because he was that future president's teacher.

THE SIGNERS

I. MASSACHUSETTS

The place where the Pilgrims settled, the site of America's oldest college (Harvard), and the birthplace of Thanksgiving and America's public school system, Massachusetts had 250,000 people by 1775. That sounds paltry today, but back then when all thirteen colonies together had only about two and a half million people, Massachusetts was the third most populous colony, trailing only Virginia and Pennsylvania. Boston, the Massachusetts capital then as now, had about 16,000 people in the mid-1770s. That would make it only a small town today, but America's only larger cities at the time were Philadelphia and New York. Massachusetts people worked at farming, fishing, shipbuilding, and, in the towns, shopkeeping.

Starting in the 1760s, Massachusetts became known as the most rebellious of the thirteen colonies, and Samuel Adams of Boston was considered the most rebellious American. In 1770 five Americans, including a black man named Crispus Attucks, were killed in a street fight with British soldiers. Samuel Adams named this clash the Boston Massacre and used it to stir up hatred against the British. Three years later Samuel Adams organized the Boston Tea Party. And the Revolution began when the British tried to capture Samuel Adams and his friend John Hancock in Lexington, Massachusetts.

Besides Samuel Adams and John Hancock, Massachusetts' other signers were Samuel's cousin John Adams, Robert Treat Paine, and Elbridge Gerry. Later, Hancock, Samuel Adams, and Gerry all served as governor of the Bay State; Paine was its first attorney general; and John Adams served as the second president of the country he had helped to create.

MASSACHUSETTS

Name	*Birth Date*	*Age at Signing*	*Marriage(s)*	*Children*	*Death Date*	*Age at Death*
Samuel Adams	September 27, 1722	53	Elizabeth Checkley Betsy Wells	6	October 2, 1803	81
John Hancock	January 12, 1737	39	Dolly Quincy	2	October 8, 1793	56
John Adams	October 30, 1735	40	Abigail Smith	5	July 4, 1826	90
Robert Treat Paine	March 11, 1731	45	Sally Cobb	8	May 11, 1814	83
Elbridge Gerry	July 17, 1744	32	Ann Thompson	10	November 23, 1814	70

Note: "Children" refers to the total number of children each signer was known to have fathered by his wife (or wives if married more than once).

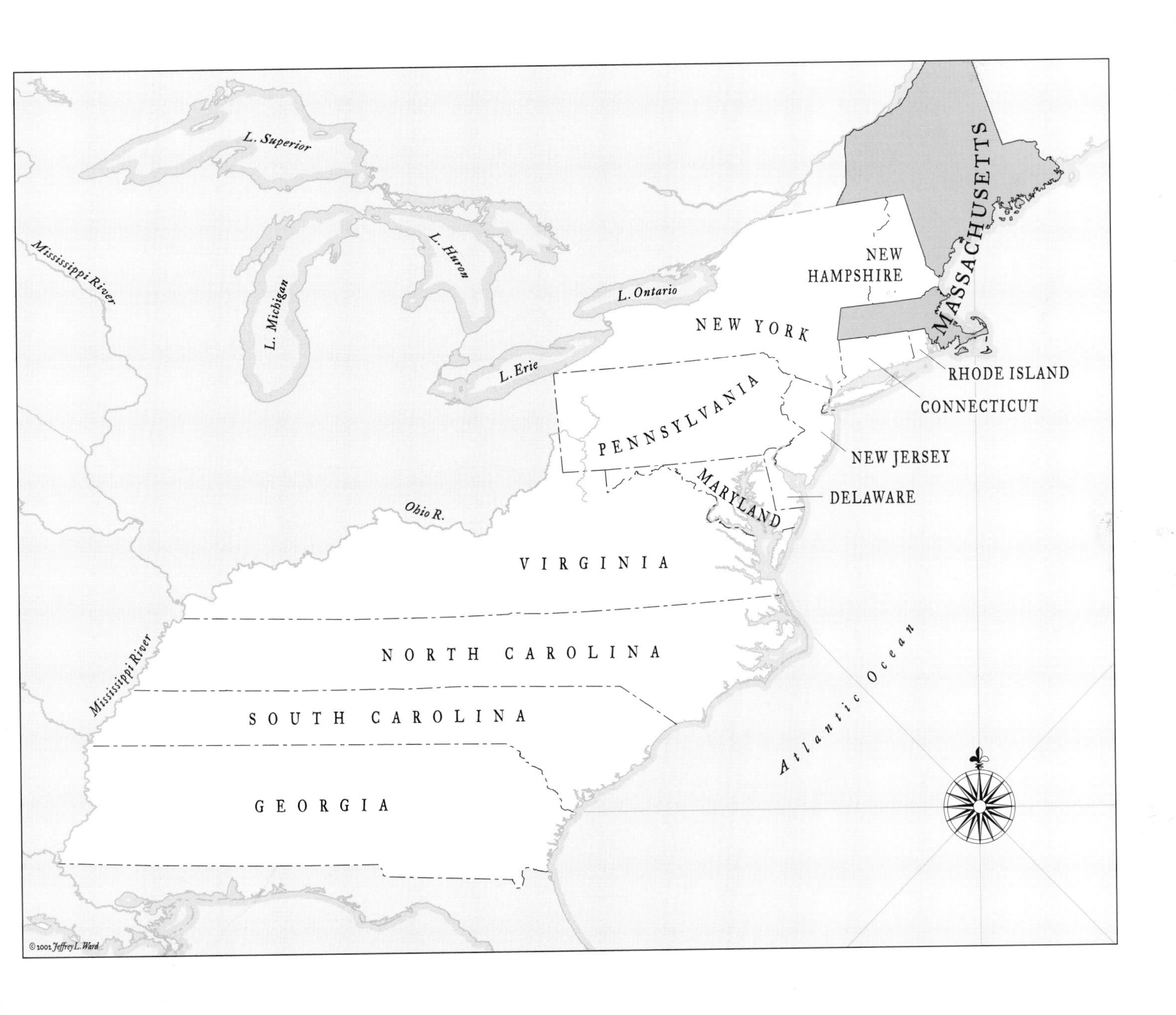

SAMUEL ADAMS:
"The Father of American Independence"

More than anyone else, a Massachusetts man ignited America's rebellion against England. In fact, during the decade before the war began, Samuel Adams was basically a one-man revolution.

He was born in Boston in 1722. Despite graduating from Harvard, Samuel failed at nearly everything he tried for many years. He went to work at a Boston countinghouse—a business similar to a bank. Samuel lost that job because he spent his time talking politics. His father gave him a large sum of money to start any business he wanted. Samuel passed along half the money to a needy friend, and he somehow lost the other half. The bottom line was that all the money was soon gone. His father then put Samuel to work in the family brewery. Samuel neglected the business until it was eventually destroyed.

Bostonians elected Samuel to the job of tax collector. People who wanted to avoid paying their taxes could not have picked a better man! As he listened to his neighbors' tales of woe about their financial problems, he felt sorry for them, and ended up collecting little of the money.

Samuel had six children with his first wife, Elizabeth Checkley. After she died, he married Betsy Wells, with whom he didn't have any children. It was said that Samuel Adams was so poor that his family would have starved had not the rich merchant John Hancock helped support them.

There was one thing that no one could do as well as Samuel Adams. By the 1760s, he was the most outspoken critic of England. He and Patrick Henry of Virginia both argued in favor of independence by about 1765 and are considered the first Americans to do so. But while Patrick made speeches, Samuel wrote thousands of letters about British injustice, which he sent to newspapers and colonial leaders around the country. He signed the newspaper letters with dozens of false names. This gave readers the impression that all of Boston was up in arms—when really just Samuel Adams was doing much of the complaining!

Samuel also recruited young men and turned them into revolutionaries. Paul Revere, Samuel's cousin John Adams, and John Hancock all considered Samuel their "political father," as Revere expressed it. All three became more famous than their political father. That was fine with Samuel Adams, who liked to remain in the shadows and let others receive the credit.

Samuel Adams took part in some of the main events that sparked the Revolution. He organized Boston's Sons of Liberty, a group of rebels who protested British injustice by destroying British property and picking fights with British officials. Dozens of towns throughout the thirteen colonies formed Sons of Liberty organizations modeled after the famous group in Boston. After England

passed a tax on tea, Samuel planned the Boston Tea Party and gave the signal for the tea to be destroyed. He also began the Committees of Correspondence, the letter-writing networks through which colonial leaders kept in touch.

The British called Samuel Adams "the Grand Incendiary," meaning someone who stirs up trouble, and "the most dangerous man in Massachusetts." The Revolution began when the British marched to Lexington, Massachusetts, in an attempt to arrest Samuel Adams and John Hancock. Fortunately, Paul Revere warned Adams and Hancock of the enemy's approach, allowing them to slip away. Soon after the war began, the British offered to pardon all Americans who would "lay down their arms and return to the duties of peaceable subjects" except for two persons: Samuel Adams and John Hancock. Had Britain won the war, the pair probably would have been among the first Americans executed.

But America triumphed, and a grateful nation called Samuel Adams "the Father of American Independence" and "the Father of the Revolution." Thomas Jefferson called him "truly the Man of the Revolution."

Later in life, Adams served as governor of the new state of Massachusetts from 1793 to 1797. Following his death, his deeds were largely forgotten, and he faded back into the shadows. He wouldn't have minded, for he often said that he worked not for personal glory but so that "millions yet unborn" could enjoy independence.

JOHN HANCOCK:
Put Your "John Hancock" Here

PEOPLE WHO ARE ABOUT TO SIGN important papers are often asked to "put your John Hancock here." The first person to sign the Declaration of Independence inspired this expression.

John Hancock was born in Braintree, Massachusetts, in 1737. His father, a minister, died when John was seven. The family had more than their grief to contend with. Their home was reserved for the minister, so they had to move out to make room for the new preacher. John's mother couldn't afford to keep the family together. She and her other two children moved in with Grandfather Hancock in Lexington, Massachusetts, while John went to live with his wealthy uncle Thomas and aunt Lydia Hancock in their mansion on Boston's Beacon Hill.

His aunt and uncle, who had no children of their own, showered John with love and everything that money could buy, including a Harvard education. John adored them, too, but all his life he was haunted by being separated from his mother, brother, and sister.

Following college graduation, John went to work for Uncle Thomas. In 1764 Thomas Hancock died, leaving most of his fortune to his nephew. Suddenly, at twenty-seven, John Hancock was one of the richest people in Massachusetts.

John enjoyed his wealth. He owned enough suits to open a clothing store, drove about in a fancy carriage, and gave parties that were the talk of Boston. He also used his money for the public good, which made him very popular. For example, he helped rebuild damaged structures after a fire, and every winter he donated food to poor Bostonians.

Samuel Adams decided to recruit Hancock for the Liberty Party, as the radicals were called. He took Hancock to his political meetings and convinced him to join the patriot cause. They were an odd couple—Adams in his threadbare suit accompanied by the dashing young merchant. At Samuel's prodding, John ran for office, and in 1766 he was elected to the Massachusetts legislature.

Hancock poured his heart, soul—and money—into the patriot cause. He gave so much money to the rebels that Bostonians joked, "Samuel Adams writes the letters [to the newspapers], and John Hancock pays the postage." Hancock was also the central figure in a famous act of defiance. In May 1768 his ship, *Liberty,*

entered Boston Harbor. A British tax man climbed aboard to inspect the vessel. By Hancock's order, the crew locked him in a cabin. John Hancock was arrested, but his lawyer, John Adams, managed to have the charges dropped. However, the British seized the *Liberty* and never returned it to him. In 1774 he further enraged the British by making a speech in which he suggested that the colonists form an independent nation called the United States of America—one of the first times this name was proposed.

As war approached, Hancock was elected president of a new Massachusetts government that was the forerunner of its state government. Under Hancock, Massachusetts raised bands of "minutemen." These soldiers, who claimed they could get ready to fight in sixty seconds, were soon needed. On the morning of April 19, 1775, British troops came to capture Hancock and Samuel Adams, who were hiding in Lexington. Thanks to Paul Revere's famous ride, Hancock and Adams were warned. A little-known fact is that Samuel had a tough time convincing John to flee. Hancock wanted to join the minutemen who fought the Battle of Lexington on the village green, beginning the Revolutionary War.

John Hancock and Samuel Adams soon headed to Philadelphia for the Second Continental Congress. In May 1775, Hancock was elected president of Congress. Three months later Hancock married Dolly Quincy, with whom he would have two children. Their daughter, Lydia, lived less than a year. Their other child, John George Washington Hancock, hit his head while ice skating and died at the age of eight.

As president of the Continental Congress, John Hancock was the first person to sign the Declaration of Independence. Reportedly, while signing in large, bold letters on July 4, 1776, Hancock said, "There! John Bull [a nickname for England] can read my name without spectacles and may double his reward on my head!"

Hancock was immensely popular with the American patriots after signing the Declaration. In 1780 he was elected the first state governor of Massachusetts in a landslide. He served as governor for a total of eleven years, but suffered so severely from a painful disease called gout that at times he couldn't walk and had to be carried about Boston. He was still governor of the Bay State when he died in 1793 at the age of fifty-six.

JOHN ADAMS:
"Survive or Perish with My Country"

John Adams

TWO SIGNERS WENT ON TO BECOME PRESIDENT of the new nation. The first was John Adams of Massachusetts.

Born in Braintree (today Quincy), near Boston, in 1735, John graduated from Harvard, then taught school for a year. Although he later claimed that he learned all that he needed to know about human nature from his students, he was not very fond of teaching, so he turned to the study of law. Just after he became an attorney, he met Abigail Smith. He and "Miss Adorable," as he called her, were married in 1764. The couple had five children and enjoyed a lifelong love affair that ended only with her death after fifty-four years of marriage. The many letters John and Abigail Adams exchanged when apart provide us with a vivid picture of revolutionary times.

Like many other young men, John was led to the patriot cause by his cousin Samuel Adams. In 1770 John was elected to the Massachusetts legislature, where he and Samuel spearheaded the fight against English oppression. John served in the Continental Congress from 1774 to 1777. One of the hardest-working congressmen, he awoke at four each morning and kept going until ten at night. By 1775 he believed that America must become independent. "The die is now cast," he wrote in a letter. "Sink or swim, live or die, survive or perish with my country is my unalterable determination."

Thanks partly to John's efforts, the new nation survived. In Congress, he and his cousin were instrumental in appointing George Washington to command the Continental Army. As a member of the committee assigned to draft the Declaration, he convinced Thomas Jefferson to do the writing. Years later, Adams described his discussion with Jefferson about it:

TJ: "You should do it!"

JA: "Oh! No."

TJ: "Why will you not? You ought to do it."

JA: "I will not."

TJ: "Why?"

JA: "Reasons enough."

TJ: "What can be your reasons?"

JA: "Reason first—you are a Virginian, and a Virginian ought to appear at the head of this business. Reason second—I am obnoxious, suspected, and unpopular. You are very much otherwise. Reason third—you can write ten times better than I can."

TJ: "Well, if you are decided, I will do as well as I can."

John Adams and Benjamin Franklin made a few minor changes in Jefferson's stirring document that called a new nation to arms. John Adams put his "John Hancock" on the Declaration right below his cousin Samuel's signature.

Early in 1778, Congress sent John Adams to obtain help for America in France. John and Abigail decided that their ten-year-old son, John Quincy Adams, should go, too. John and John Quincy Adams were at sea when their ship engaged in a battle with a British vessel. John grabbed his musket and went out on deck with his young son. Suddenly a cannonball slammed into the ship near where the father and son were standing. Had it struck a few feet away, it might have killed two future U.S. presidents.

Following the Revolution, John Adams helped negotiate the peace treaty. He later served his country in many ways. In the first election for president in 1789, George Washington received the most votes; John Adams came in second. By the method then used, Washington became president and Adams vice president. Then in 1796 John Adams was elected as the nation's second president. He held the office from 1797 until 1801.

Abigail didn't live long enough to see it, but John Adams was still alive when his son John Quincy Adams took office as the nation's sixth president in 1825. Until George and George W. Bush, John and John Quincy Adams were the only father and son to both hold the nation's highest office.

John Adams remained vigorous until his late eighties, walking three miles a day. By a remarkable coincidence, John Adams and Thomas Jefferson died on the same day—July 4, 1826, precisely fifty years after the adoption of the Declaration of Independence. The last words uttered by the ninety-year-old John Adams were, "Thomas Jefferson still survives," but unknown to Adams, the author of the Declaration of Independence had died a few hours earlier.

ROBERT TREAT PAINE:
He Was No Angel

SOMETIMES WE FORGET that the signers were real people with flaws. When we do that, we should think of Robert Treat Paine.

Bob, as he was called, was born in Boston in 1731. He entered Harvard at fourteen, graduated at eighteen, and then taught school in the Massachusetts town of Lunenburg. Paine soon discovered that he lacked the patience to teach. In a letter to his sister Abigail, he wrote: "I began my school. O how [the students] did hum & haw & whine & sing & every thing else disagreeable."

Paine taught until he couldn't take it anymore (about a year) and then went to sea. Over the next few years he sailed to such places as North Carolina, Spain, and the Azores, a group of islands belonging to Portugal. His final voyage in 1754 was a whaling trip to Greenland.

Back home, Paine had to decide on a new career. From entries in his diary we know that he sometimes got drunk and that he had what he called a "Stray Heart," meaning that he had a number of romances. He finally settled on a legal career and became a lawyer in Taunton, Massachusetts. He married Sally Cobb, who was already pregnant with their first child, in 1770. Bob and Sally would have a total of eight children.

Also in 1770, Paine took on a major case: The town of Boston hired him to prosecute the British soldiers accused of killing five Americans in the Boston Massacre. Although all the soldiers were found not guilty or got off with light sentences, Paine made a name for himself among the patriots. In 1773 he was elected from Taunton to the Massachusetts legislature, and the next year he was sent to the Continental Congress. Some congressmen considered him difficult to work with. In fact, he was nicknamed "the Objection Maker" because he seemed to oppose every measure that he didn't propose himself. Although not as eager for independence as Samuel or John Adams, Robert Treat Paine signed the Declaration with his "scrawl," as he called his terrible handwriting.

From 1777 to 1790 Paine served as the first attorney general of the state of Massachusetts. He then served as a judge for fourteen years, until he was too deaf to hear cases, becoming more conservative with age. One of his and Sally's children, Robert Treat Paine Jr., was a well-known poet who became involved in the theater and married an actress. In those days, some old-timers like Samuel Adams and Robert Treat Paine considered the theater harmful to the morals of Americans. Sadly, Robert Treat Paine, who hadn't been an angel himself when young, refused to have anything more to do with his son because of his marriage to the actress. His son became an alcoholic and drifted into poverty. Only after many years did the father and son make up. The thirty-seven-year-old poet died in his parents' attic room in 1811. Robert Treat Paine, the signer, died three years later, at the age of eighty-three.

ELBRIDGE GERRY:
Fiery Little Marbleheader

Elbridge Gerry

JOHN ADAMS ONCE WROTE that if his fellow congressmen were all like Elbridge Gerry, "the Liberties of America would be safe."

Gerry was born in the seaside town of Marblehead, Massachusetts, in 1744. He entered Harvard at fourteen—very young by today's standards but not unusual for the few colonists who attended college. To receive his master's degree from Harvard in 1765, Gerry had to present an argument on a subject. Twenty-year-old Elbridge Gerry argued that Americans should resist the British Stamp Act, a tax on paper goods that had been passed that year.

Gerry then returned home and joined his family's merchant business. In 1772 Marbleheaders (as people from his town were called) elected Gerry to the Massachusetts colonial legislature, where he met Samuel Adams. Seeing that Gerry had the patriotic spark, the "Grand Incendiary" took him under his wing and encouraged him to become even more rebellious. The fiery little Marbleheader who stuttered when speaking became one of his colony's leading revolutionaries, among other things helping to gather military supplies and distribute them to Massachusetts minutemen.

On the night of April 18, 1775, Gerry attended a meeting of patriots in what is now Arlington, Massachusetts. Afterward, he and two colleagues went to sleep in the town's Black Horse Tavern. During the night they were awakened by the sound of British troops marching to what would be the opening battles of the Revolution at Lexington and Concord. To avoid capture, Gerry and his two friends ran outside and hid in a cornfield just before some soldiers entered the tavern to search it. The three men lay on the cold ground in their nightclothes until the soldiers were gone. One of Gerry's companions became ill from exposure and soon died.

A few months later Gerry was elected to the Continental Congress. Taking his seat in February 1776, he became known as one of the boldest spokesmen for independence. Gerry signed the Declaration in September, and forever after considered it the crowning achievement of his life.

Elbridge Gerry remained a bachelor until the age of forty-one. In 1786 he married Ann Thompson, who was twenty years younger than he. The couple, who settled in a mansion in Cambridge, Massachusetts, had ten children.

While serving as governor of Massachusetts from 1810 to 1812, Elbridge Gerry helped enact a law dividing the Bay State into political districts favorable to

his own party. This resulted in some odd-shaped districts. One district looked like a salamander, someone said. Someone else joked that it looked more like a "gerrymander," making a play on the governor's name. To this day, the practice of drawing boundary lines to favor a political party or group is called gerrymandering.

In 1812 Elbridge Gerry was elected vice president of the United States under President James Madison. Gerry was serving in the nation's second highest office when he died suddenly, perhaps of a heart attack, on November 23, 1814, in Washington, D.C. His widow was the last surviving wife of a signer to die. Ann Gerry lived until 1849—seventy-three years after her husband's proudest moment, when he signed the Declaration of Independence.

II. VIRGINIA

Virginia was the site of England's first permanent American town—Jamestown—which was founded in 1607. One of Jamestown's leaders was Captain John Smith, whose life was saved by the Native American girl Pocahontas in a story that became part of American lore. Another "first" occurred in 1619, when the Virginia legislature, called the House of Burgesses—the first lawmaking body in the thirteen colonies composed of elected representatives—met in Jamestown. The College of William and Mary was established in Williamsburg in 1693. Today it is the nation's second-oldest college, behind only Harvard. In 1699 Williamsburg became Virginia's capital, which it remained until the end of colonial times.

Relatively few colonial Virginians lived in Williamsburg and other towns, however. Most were farmers. Its inhabitants grew so much tobacco that Virginia was nicknamed "the tobacconized colony." While many of the colony's settlers lived in log homes and grew their own crops, wealthy Virginians lived on magnificent estates called plantations, where slaves did the work. By 1775 Virginia was by far the most populous of the thirteen colonies, with 500,000 people, nearly half of them black slaves.

Only Massachusetts was a more rebellious colony than Virginia. Although he wasn't a signer, Virginia patriot Patrick Henry made a famous speech in which he emphatically declared, "Give me liberty or give me death!" One of Virginia's seven signers, Richard Henry Lee, proposed independence in Congress, and another, Thomas Jefferson, wrote the Declaration of Independence.

VIRGINIA

Name	*Birth Date*	*Age at Signing*	*Marriage(s)*	*Children*	*Death Date*	*Age at Death*
Richard Henry Lee	Probably January 1733	Probably 43	Anne Aylett Anne Pinckard	9	June 19, 1794	Probably 61
Francis Lightfoot Lee	October 14, 1734	41	Rebecca Tayloe	0	Early 1797	62
George Wythe	1726	About 50	Ann Lewis Elizabeth Taliaferro	1	June 8, 1806	About 80
Thomas Jefferson	April 13, 1743	33	Martha Skelton	6	July 4, 1826	83
Thomas Nelson	December 26, 1738	37	Lucy Grymes	13	January 4, 1789	50
Carter Braxton	September 10, 1736	39	Judith Robinson Elizabeth Corbin	18	October 10, 1797	61
Benjamin Harrison	1726	About 50	Elizabeth Bassett	7	April 24, 1791	About 65

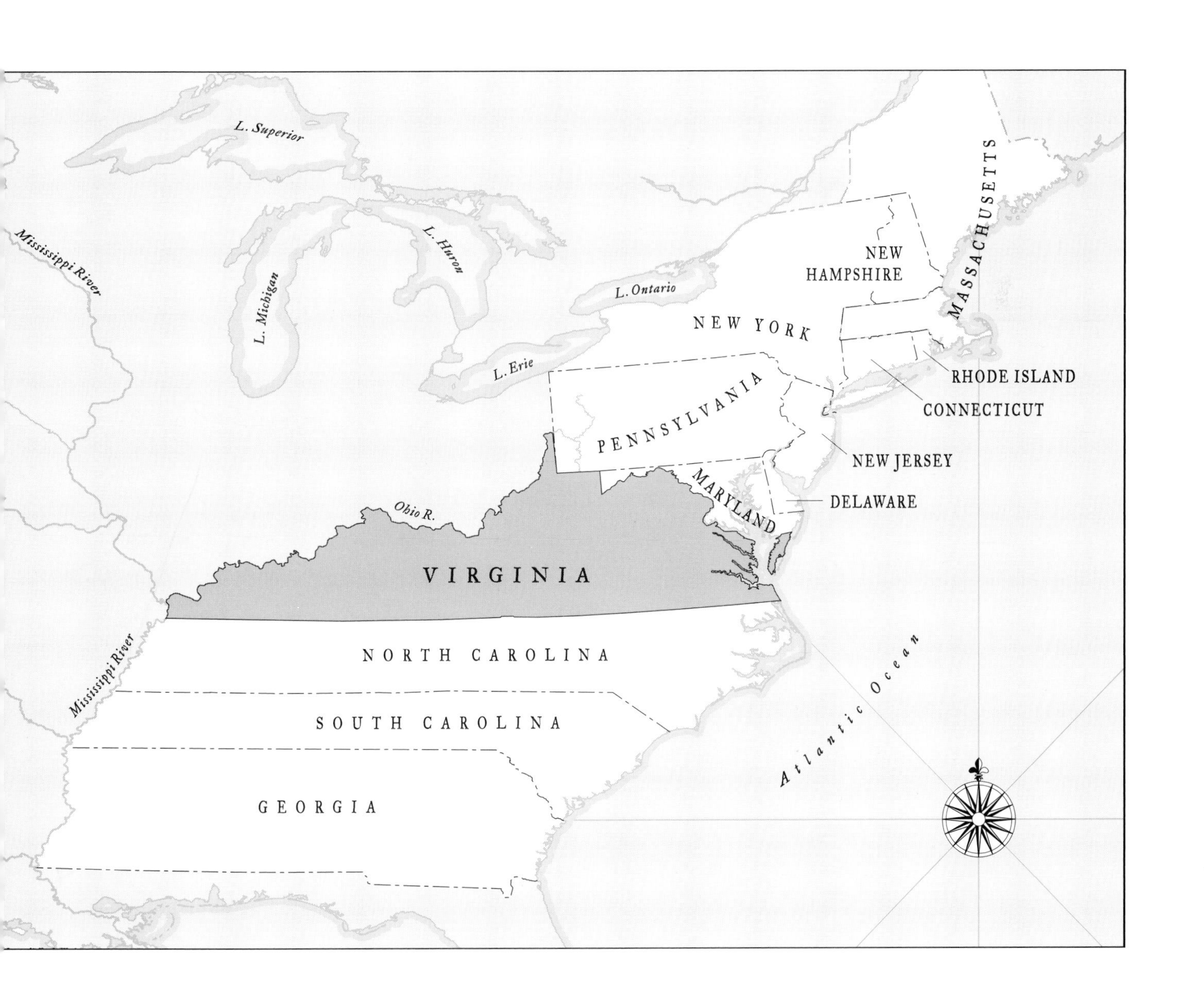

RICHARD HENRY LEE:

"Free and Independent States"

Richard Henry Lee

VIRGINIA HAD THE ONLY PAIR OF BROTHERS who signed the Declaration. The older of the two had the honor of proposing that Congress declare independence.

Richard Henry Lee, the seventh of eleven children, was born in Virginia's Westmoreland County. Some authorities say he was born in 1732, but the Lee family Bible reveals that his birth date was more likely in January 1733. His family had their own schoolhouse on their estate, where tutors taught the children. At age eleven, Richard Henry was sent to England. For seven years he studied in the mother country and then traveled through Europe for a few months before returning home when he was eighteen.

The Lee family was so rich that Richard Henry didn't need to get a job. For a few years he whiled away his time reading and attending parties at neighboring plantations. In his mid-twenties he married Anne Aylett. The couple had four children and established an estate, Chantilly, on the Potomac River. The year 1768 was disastrous for Richard Henry Lee and his family. That spring he blew off four fingers in a hunting accident, and in December his wife died. Richard Henry Lee later married Anne Pinckard, with whom he had another five children.

The Lees had been active in Virginia politics as far back as the 1640s. Following the family tradition, Richard Henry Lee was elected to Virginia's legislature, the House of Burgesses, in 1758, and served for the next seventeen years.

Lee was one of the first Virginia lawmakers to favor independence. When Britain closed the port of Boston as punishment for the Boston Tea Party, Lee was one of the Virginia leaders who decided to spend June 1, 1774—the day the port closing began—in prayer and fasting. An attack on Massachusetts was an attack on all thirteen colonies, Lee insisted. This was a major step in uniting the colonies against England.

In 1774 Richard Henry Lee was sent to the Continental Congress, where he served for about five years, not counting interruptions. He was one of the best speakers in Congress. His great moment came on June 7, 1776, when he made the historic proposal "that these United Colonies are, and of right ought to be, free and independent States." Ironically, perhaps because of a family illness, Lee had to return home and missed the July 2 vote for his own proposal. However, he returned in late August and signed the famous document that he had helped bring to life. The next year, in 1777, Richard Henry Lee failed to get enough votes in Virginia to retain his seat in the Continental Congress. But a month later he was elected to fill a vacancy in Virginia's congressional delegation.

From late 1784 to late 1785 Lee was president of Congress. This made him in effect president of the United States, although of course George Washington, who was the first president under the U.S. Constitution, is considered the first person to hold the nation's highest office as we know it today. Then in 1789 Richard Henry Lee was elected as one of Virginia's first two U.S. senators. He served until 1792, when he resigned because of illness and injuries suffered in a carriage accident. Richard Henry Lee died at his home, Chantilly, in his early sixties.

FRANCIS LIGHTFOOT LEE:
The Quiet Brother

Francis Lightfoot Lee

IT WAS SAID THAT, in his quiet way, Francis Lightfoot Lee was even more strongly for independence than his older brother.

Soon after his birth in Virginia's Westmoreland County in 1734, his family moved to an estate called Stratford, where he grew up. Francis Lightfoot Lee was very wealthy, but his early life was sad. By his middle teens, he had lost both his parents.

Francis Lightfoot Lee was elected to Virginia's House of Burgesses in 1758—the same year as his brother Richard Henry. When Francis Lightfoot took his seat, he was one of five Lees in the House, including two of his brothers and two of their cousins. In 1769 Francis Lightfoot Lee married another cousin, Rebecca Tayloe. The couple had no children, but helped raise two of their nieces.

In 1775 Francis Lightfoot Lee was sent to the Continental Congress, where he once again joined his older brother, Richard Henry. The brothers were opposites in many ways. A captivating speaker, Richard Henry Lee was often the center of attention in Congress. Francis Lightfoot Lee preferred to stay in the background, working quietly on congressional committees. As a member of the Board of War, he played a vital role in obtaining supplies for the American army.

On July 2, 1776, Francis Lightfoot Lee cast his vote in favor of his brother's independence proposal, then signed the Declaration in August. The Lee brothers usually stuck together. When Richard Henry was ousted from the Virginia delegation to Congress in 1777, Francis Lightfoot gave up his seat in protest. Only after his protest helped reinstate his brother in the Virginia delegation did Francis Lightfoot return to Congress. Later the brothers resigned from Congress on the same day—May 15, 1779. However, Richard Henry later returned to

Congress and was elected its president. Francis Lightfoot served briefly in the new Virginia state legislature and then retired from public life.

A rare time that the Lee brothers disagreed occurred in 1787, over the U.S. Constitution. Richard Henry opposed this new governmental framework for the nation, while Francis Lightfoot favored it. Virginia followed Francis Lightfoot's recommendation, approving the Constitution on June 25, 1788. That day Virginia became our tenth state.

The shy signer who had quietly worked for independence died in 1797 at the age of sixty-two. Leesburg, Virginia, was named in honor of the state's renowned Lee family.

GEORGE WYTHE:
Teacher of Presidents

George Wythe

Although often overlooked today, in his own time George Wythe was the most respected of the twenty-seven signers who were lawyers.

Wythe was born in 1726 near Hampton, Virginia. His father died when George was three. In an age when girls generally had little if any schooling, George's mother was highly educated and taught him at home.

At sixteen George began to study law with his uncle, and at twenty he passed the attorney's test. The next year he married Ann Lewis, who died eight months after their wedding. Later he married Elizabeth Taliaferro, with whom he had one child who didn't survive infancy.

George Wythe won fame for his legal skill and honesty. He wouldn't take a case if he felt his client was in the wrong, and if he caught a client lying, he dropped the case and returned any fees he had been paid. Some people even poked fun at him because he preferred to lose a case than bend the truth.

Wythe was elected to the House of Burgesses in 1754 and as mayor of Williamsburg in 1768. He also taught law, eventually becoming a professor at the College of William and Mary in Williamsburg. His pupils included two future presidents, Thomas Jefferson and James Monroe. The childless Wythe sometimes paid for the schooling of needy law students and took them into his home to live. Thomas Jefferson, who had lost his father when he was just fourteen, called Wythe "my second father."

During the troubles with England, George Wythe's influence helped draw Virginia toward independence. He was elected to the Continental Congress in 1775 but was at home in Virginia when independence was approved on July 2, 1776. Either someone signed the Declaration for him in his absence, or he signed himself after returning to Congress around September 14. He served in Congress for a few more months, then returned home to revise Virginia's laws with the help of his ex-student Thomas Jefferson.

In 1788 Wythe was elected to serve in the convention in Richmond that considered whether to approve the U.S. Constitution. Wythe helped sway enough delegates—some of whom were his former students—for Virginia to narrowly give its approval and become the tenth state.

Wythe had grown to hate slavery, and after his second wife, Elizabeth, died in the late 1780s, he freed some of his slaves. In his old age he lived with two of his former slaves: his housekeeper, Lydia Broadnax, and a youth named Michael Brown. Wythe was very fond of Michael, and named him to inherit part of his estate. Also in the household was George Wythe Sweeney, the signer's great-nephew. Sweeney, who was in line to inherit most of Wythe's estate, ran up gambling debts. First he forged his uncle's name on checks. Then, to get the whole estate, he poured poison into coffee that George Wythe, Michael Brown, and Lydia Broadnax drank. The signer and young Brown died, but Lydia, although gravely ill, survived.

There was plenty of evidence against Sweeney, but by Virginia law blacks couldn't testify against whites in court, so Lydia wasn't heard, and Sweeney was found not guilty of murder. George Wythe, the signer who was dear to Thomas Jefferson and so many others, was about eighty years old when he was murdered in 1806.

THOMAS JEFFERSON:
"All Men Are Created Equal"

Th Jefferson

A YOUNG REDHEAD FROM VIRGINIA wrote the paper that is sometimes referred to as the birth certificate of the United States.

Thomas Jefferson was born at Shadwell, a plantation in Virginia's Albemarle County, in 1743. His youth was divided between Shadwell, which was at the edge of the wilderness, and a large estate that his father managed in eastern Virginia.

Thomas had the best of two worlds. On the frontier, where his neighbors were poor farmers, he swam, fished, hunted, and rode through the countryside. While living near the coast, he learned to dance, play the violin, and conduct himself like an English gentleman. Wherever he was, he spent many hours curled up with a book.

His father died when Thomas was fourteen and he inherited about 2,500 acres (about four square miles) of land and about thirty slaves. Two years later he entered the College of William and Mary, astonishing his professors with his keen interest in *everything*. After graduating at the age of nineteen, he studied law with George Wythe. On New Year's Day of 1772 the young lawyer married Martha Skelton, with whom he had six children, only two of whom lived to adulthood.

At twenty-six, Jefferson was elected to Virginia's House of Burgesses. He spoke out about the colonists' right to self-rule, leading to his selection as a delegate to the Second Continental Congress in 1775. His gift for writing won him the honor of creating the Declaration of Independence. In his apartment at Market and Seventh Streets in Philadelphia he began writing, "When in the course of human events it becomes necessary for one people to dissolve the political bands which have connected them with another . . ." He used no reference books while writing the Declaration in two weeks of late June. Instead, Jefferson mixed his own ideas and phrases with ones he recalled from his extensive reading.

Like all writers, Jefferson had to submit his work for editing. In his case he had approximately fifty editors—the members of Congress. Their editorial changes stung Jefferson. Nevertheless, most historians believe that the changes in wording made by Benjamin Franklin, John Adams, and others improved the Declaration.

One of Jefferson's favorite sayings was, "It is wonderful how much may be done if we are always doing." He lived by that motto, achieving much in an incredible number of fields. A brilliant architect, he designed his famous home, Monticello, as well as the state capitol building in Richmond (which replaced Williamsburg as the Virginia capital in 1780). A strong believer in education, he founded the University of Virginia. He was nicknamed "Mr. Mammoth" because he collected prehistoric bones. He has been called America's "first serious gardener" and the "father of American forestry" because of his passion

for planting flowers and trees. He was one of America's best violinists of his time. His inventions included a new kind of plow, an improved sundial, and a cipher wheel, a device that helped him send coded messages while he was a diplomat in France. In addition, his library became the basis for the nation's Library of Congress.

Besides all this, he served his country in many ways. He was governor of Virginia, U.S. minister to France, and the country's first secretary of state under President George Washington. Thomas Jefferson was the nation's vice president from 1797 to 1801 under President John Adams. Then, from 1801 to 1809 he held the nation's highest office, serving as the third president of the United States. He was one of eight presidents who were born in Virginia, which became known as the Mother of Presidents.

Thomas Jefferson felt guilty about one aspect of his life. He had asserted in the Declaration of Independence that "all men are created equal" and are entitled to "Life, Liberty, and the pursuit of Happiness." Yet he was a big slaveholder, owning a total of approximately 400 African-Americans at one time or another at Monticello. Jefferson seems to have been tormented by the fact that he professed one thing about everyone's right to liberty while practicing another. He also kept secret the fact that he fathered children by one of his slaves. In addition to his six children by his wife, Martha, Jefferson had several children with Sally Hemings, a slave at Monticello. As a result, there is an African-American branch of Jefferson's family to this day.

The author of the Declaration of Independence lived to the age of eighty-three, dying, like John Adams, on the fiftieth anniversary of the adoption of the famous document. Jefferson is pictured on the front of the United States's five-cent piece, or nickel, and his home, Monticello, is shown on the back of the coin.

THOMAS NELSON:
He Had His Own Tea Party

Thos Nelson jr.

Colonial Americans lived to an average age of less than forty—roughly half of today's typical life span. Smallpox, high blood pressure, complications from childbirth, and other problems that medicine has learned to deal with claimed thousands of lives. Despite suffering from poor health for many years, the Virginia signer performed some remarkable deeds for his country.

Thomas Nelson was born into one of colonial America's wealthiest families in Yorktown on the day after Christmas of 1738. His father twice served as Virginia's acting governor. At fourteen, Tom was sent to England, where he attended school. A prominent name meant so much in his time that Nelson was elected to the House of Burgesses while he was still on the ship sailing home—even though he was just twenty-two years old and had been away for eight years. The next year, 1762, he married Lucy Grymes, a talented harpsichord player with whom he would have thirteen children.

Thomas's father died in 1772, leaving him 20,000 acres of land and more than 400 slaves. Two years later, Nelson performed a daring protest against the British Tea Act: He boarded the ship *Virginia,* anchored near his home in Yorktown, and dumped two chests of British tea into the York River. This was very risky in an age when destroying another person's property was a serious crime. Even Samuel Adams, the organizer of the Boston Tea Party, hadn't taken part in the actual tea dumping. Nelson seems to have escaped punishment for his bold act of defiance.

Thomas Nelson was elected to the Continental Congress in the summer of 1775. One of the first congressmen to favor complete separation from England, he placed his John Hancock on the Declaration in August 1776. The following spring in Congress, at the age of only thirty-eight, he suffered a stroke that affected his memory. He returned home and recovered somewhat, but he apparently had subsequent strokes and also suffered from periodic bouts of asthma.

Amazingly, Thomas Nelson kept going. He held a seat in Virginia's legislature during the war and raised money, sometimes using his own funds, to pay troops. In 1781 he served as Virginia's governor. Most remarkable of all, he became a wartime general.

In the fall of 1781, General Nelson led 3,000 Virginia militiamen as part of George Washington's forces at Yorktown, Virginia. British soldiers had taken refuge in the Nelson home in Yorktown. Although Nelson's family was not inside, the American troops refused to fire at the house. According to a famous story, General Nelson angrily asked the American gunners, "Why do you spare my house?"

"Out of respect to you," came the answer.

"Give me the cannon!" Nelson reportedly yelled. At his direction, his own home was bombarded and hit several times.

The British surrendered at Yorktown on October 19, 1781, marking the end of major Revolutionary War fighting. Thomas Nelson had sacrificed his health and a fortune to help win independence. He died in early 1789, nine days after his fiftieth birthday.

CARTER BRAXTON:
"With One United Voice"

Carter Braxton

As the Revolution began, about a third of all Americans favored independence, a third sided with England, and a third were undecided. To win independence, the fence-sitters had to be won over, especially the undecided leaders such as Carter Braxton.

Braxton was born in 1736, near where Richmond, Virginia, would be established when he was six years old. He was named for his grandfather, Robert Carter, who was nicknamed "King Carter" because he owned forty-two plantations. Carter Braxton's cousins included two future signers, Thomas Nelson and Benjamin Harrison.

Carter's early years were marked by tragedy. His mother died at his birth. At thirteen, he lost his father. The boy was raised by family friends. At eighteen he dropped out of college to marry, but his wife, Judith Robinson Braxton, died two years later giving birth to their second child.

Within a few years, Braxton's life improved. He remarried, and with his second wife, Elizabeth Corbin Braxton, he had sixteen children. That gave Braxton a total of *eighteen* sons and daughters! By his late thirties he had settled into a prosperous and pleasant life. His numerous slaves worked his vast tracts of land, while he entered into business ventures with Robert Morris of Pennsylvania and other prominent merchants. For many years Braxton served in the House of Burgesses. And for entertainment there were the balls and parties that the wealthy Virginia planters took turns hosting.

The Revolution threatened Braxton's comfortable way of life, so for a long time he was lukewarm about independence. In late 1775 he was named to Virginia's delegation in the Continental Congress. As late as April 14, 1776, he wrote a letter to an uncle saying that America was not ready for independence.

Just a month later, on May 17, he wrote his uncle that "America with one united Voice" should seek independence. What had changed his mind? Perhaps other delegates had convinced him that the time for independence had arrived. More likely he felt it would hurt the country if Congress appeared to be divided over the issue. Carter Braxton voted for independence, signed the Declaration on August 2, and then left Congress.

Back home, he served in Virginia's new state legislature, where he presented a plan to help win the war. Slaves should be recruited to defend Virginia and granted their freedom in return, he said. Virginia rejected the idea, but eventually about 5,000 African-American men, many of them slaves, served in the patriot forces.

Braxton helped supply salt, uniforms, and blankets for the American forces that fought for independence. Partly because of the war and partly because of poor business decisions, he lost his fortune. He might have gone to debtor's prison like his business associate Robert Morris, but he suffered a stroke and died at the age of sixty-one before that could happen. Braxton County in what is now West Virginia was named for him.

BENJAMIN HARRISON:
"We Will Show Mother Britain!"

Benj Harrison

WHENEVER THE NAME Benjamin Harrison is mentioned, most people think of the twenty-third president. Few people know that President Harrison's great-grandfather Benjamin Harrison signed the Declaration of Independence.

Benjamin Harrison the signer was born in Charles City County, Virginia, in 1726. He attended the College of William and Mary at Williamsburg but left without graduating. It was said that he quarreled with a professor, but more likely he had to return home to manage his family's estate after his father was killed by lightning. Soon after, he married Elizabeth Bassett, with whom he had seven children.

Harrison was only twenty-three when he was elected to the House of Burgesses, where he served for the next quarter century. He was elected to the Continental Congress in August 1774. In Philadelphia, he shared a house with fellow Virginian George Washington. Known for his memorable remarks, Harrison told John Adams that he would have walked the 200 miles to get to Congress, if need be.

At the time John Hancock was elected president of Congress in May 1775, the British were especially enraged at Hancock's home colony, Massachusetts, which they felt had led the thirteen colonies into war. Harrison, who was six feet four and weighed 240 pounds, reportedly picked up Hancock and set him down in the president's chair while commenting, "We will show Mother Britain how little we care for her by making a Massachusetts man our president!"

As he signed the Declaration on August 2, Harrison supposedly made a famous remark to Elbridge Gerry, who was one of the smaller signers. "With me it will all be over in a minute," said Harrison, meaning that he would die quickly from the hangman's rope because of his great weight. "But you, you'll be dancing on air an hour after I'm gone." Actually, Gerry was away from Congress at the time and didn't sign until his return in September 1776, but perhaps

Harrison made this attempt at gallows humor on another day when he and Gerry were together.

While in Congress, Harrison helped establish three major governmental departments—what we now call the Defense, Navy, and State Departments. He left Congress in the fall of 1777, and from 1781 to 1784 served as governor of the new state of Virginia. Near the end of the war, his quip about the hangman's rope nearly came true. He had to flee into the interior of Virginia to avoid being captured by the English.

Benjamin Harrison the signer was the father of one president and the great-grandfather of another. William Henry Harrison, the youngest of Benjamin and Elizabeth's seven children, grew up to become the nation's ninth president. The signer's great-grandson, also named Benjamin Harrison, was our twenty-third president.

III. PENNSYLVANIA

Before becoming one of England's thirteen colonies, Pennsylvania was claimed by Sweden and the Netherlands. But by 1664, when England seized the area, fewer than 1,000 settlers lived there.

In 1681 the king of England gave a large region to William Penn, naming it Pennsylvania, meaning "Penn's woods." Penn was a Quaker, a faith that preached peace and understanding. Religious prejudice was rampant in most of the colonies, but Pennsylvania welcomed everyone. Quakers, Catholics, Jews, Lutherans, and others moved there. By 1775 Pennsylvania had about 300,000 people—the most of any colony except Virginia. Philadelphia, with 40,000 people, was the largest city in the thirteen colonies.

Pennsylvania's vote on July 2, 1776, was crucial. Besides having the largest city and hosting the Continental Congress, Pennsylvania was centrally located. If Pennsylvania remained loyal to England, America would be split in two. Pennsylvania did choose independence, but only because two of its delegates didn't vote. Angry that their colony had nearly rejected separation from England, on July 20 Pennsylvania's patriot leaders sent a revamped delegation, stacked with independence men, to Congress. The result was that Pennsylvania had nine signers, the most of any colony.

As the Declaration's birthplace, Philadelphia has some attractions relating to the document. The hall where Congress approved the Declaration is called Independence Hall. And the bell in the building's tower that was rung to announce the Declaration is known as the Liberty Bell.

PENNSYLVANIA

Name	Birth Date	Age at Signing	Marriage(s)	Children	Death Date	Age at Death
Benjamin Franklin	January 17, 1706	70	Deborah Read	2	April 17, 1790	84
Robert Morris	January 31, 1734	42	Mary White	7	May 8, 1806	72
Benjamin Rush	January 1746	30	Julia Stockton	13	April 19, 1813	67
George Clymer	March 16, 1739	37	Elizabeth Meredith	8	January 23, 1813	73
James Wilson	September 14, 1742	33	Rachel Bird Hannah Gray	7	August 21, 1798	55
John Morton	1724 or 1725	Early fifties	Ann Justis	9	April 1, 1777	About 52
George Ross	May 10, 1730	46	Anne Lawler	3	July 14, 1779	49
George Taylor	1716	About 60	Anne Savage	2	February 23, 1781	About 65
James Smith	About 1719	About 57	Eleanor Armor	5	July 11, 1806	About 87

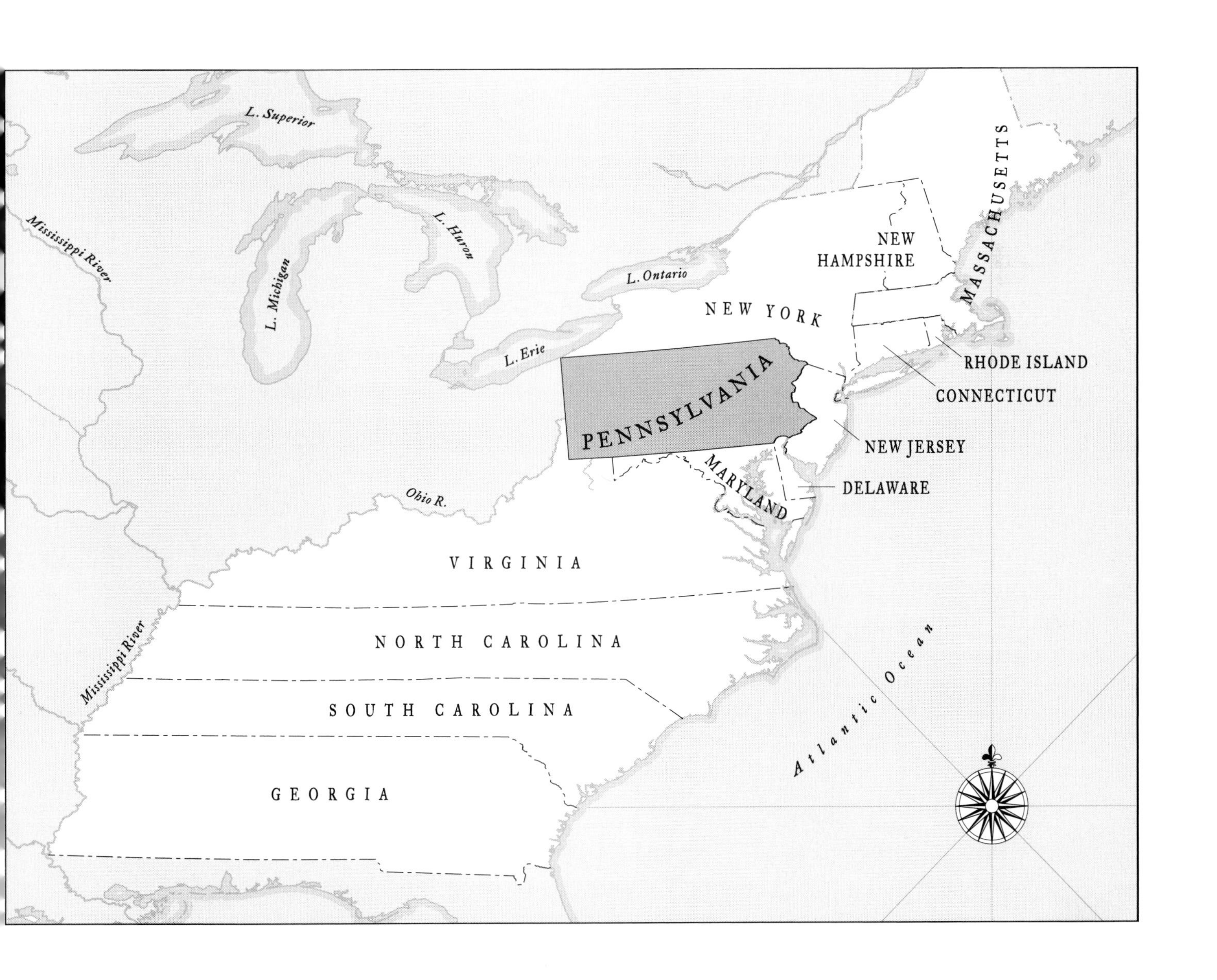

BENJAMIN FRANKLIN:
"We Must All Hang Together"

Benj. Franklin

THANKS TO HIS INVENTIONS, discoveries, and other achievements, the oldest of the fifty-six signers was also the most famous American of his time.

Born in Boston, Massachusetts, in 1706, Benjamin Franklin was the fifteenth in a family of seventeen children. From childhood, he looked for new ways to do things. One windy day he was flying a kite when he came to a pond. Ben took off his clothes, lay back in the water, and held onto the kite string. As the wind blew the kite, Ben was towed across the pond!

After just two years of school, ten-year-old Ben was put to work making candles in the family shop. He hated it. At twelve, he became an apprentice to his older brother James, who was a printer. Ben learned the printer's trade, but when he made mistakes, James hit him. Tired of the beatings, Ben ran away from home at seventeen and settled in Philadelphia.

Ben set up a printing business and in 1729 began his own newspaper, the *Pennsylvania Gazette.* A few years later he founded *Poor Richard's Almanac,* which he published between 1733 and 1758. In his almanac, he popularized many sayings, such as "Haste makes waste" and "Early to bed, and early to rise, makes a man healthy, wealthy, and wise."

Ben had married Deborah Read in 1730. Ben and Debby had a daughter, Sally, and a son, Franky, who died of smallpox when he was just four. By another woman Ben had a son named William, whom Debby treated as her own child. Debby assisted Ben with his printing business. With her help, he became America's largest bookseller, and the *Pennsylvania Gazette* became the leading newspaper.

Printing was just one of Ben's interests. Science was another. In June 1752 Ben and his son William performed a famous but risky experiment. They flew a kite in a storm. Lightning hit the kite and zoomed down the string to a key, where it made a spark. This proved that lightning was electricity. Another time, while riding through Maryland, Ben and William spotted a tornado and galloped toward it, backing away only when tree branches nearly hit them. Ben's observations provided people with a better understanding of tornadoes.

"What good is science that does not apply to some use?" Ben once asked. He invented many devices to help people. To protect human beings and property from lightning, he created the lightning rod. In addition, he invented a heating device called the Franklin stove and a type of eyeglasses called bifocals that millions of people wear today.

Ben also helped make Philadelphia a great city. He founded the Library Company of Philadelphia (a step in building America's public library system), the

Union Fire Company (America's first volunteer fire department), the Pennsylvania Hospital (the country's first general hospital), and the school that is now the University of Pennsylvania.

He found time for politics, too. Franklin served in the Pennsylvania Assembly and in the Second Continental Congress, where he helped Thomas Jefferson a little with the writing of the Declaration of Independence. At seventy, Ben was the oldest signer. He reportedly made a famous remark at the signing. John Hancock, president of Congress, said, "We must all hang together," meaning they must cooperate. "Yes," responded Ben. "We must all hang together, or most assuredly we shall all hang separately!"

During the war, Ben went overseas and convinced France to fight on his country's side, which helped turn the tide in America's favor. But the war brought a great personal blow to Ben. His son William was New Jersey's royal governor, running the colony for the king. Ben begged his son to quit and side with America. William refused and was kicked out of office by American patriots and jailed.

"Nothing ever hurt me so much," Ben said about his son siding with Britain. He and his son never made up.

In 1787, eighty-one-year-old Ben Franklin helped create the U.S. Constitution, which he also signed. He served as Pennsylvania's governor in his last years and died in 1790. After the age of seventy, Benjamin Franklin had decided that he wanted to get younger, so he had begun counting backward with each new birthday. By the usual counting system he was eighty-four, but by his own method he was only fifty-six years old when he died in 1790!

ROBERT MORRIS:
"The Financier of the Revolution"

Robt Morris

IT HAS BEEN SAID that independence couldn't have been won without three men: army commander George Washington; Benjamin Franklin, who convinced France to help America; and Robert Morris, "the Financier of the Revolution."

Robert was born in England in 1734. What became of his mother is unknown. When Robert was about four, his father sailed to America, where he worked for an English firm. At thirteen, Robert joined his father in the new country, finding employment with Philadelphia merchant Charles Willing. When his father died in a shooting accident, sixteen-year-old Robert was left alone in the world. He had to live by his wits—which he did remarkably well.

Once, while Mr. Willing was away, Robert learned that the price of flour was about to skyrocket. The teenage clerk bought up all the flour he could find in the Philadelphia area. The price of flour rose sharply the next day, netting large profits for the Willing company. Robert did so well at buying and selling goods that by the age of twenty-three he had been made a partner in a new firm called Willing & Morris, which became one of America's leading businesses. In 1769 Robert Morris married Mary White. The couple had seven children, raising their family on an estate called The Hills outside Philadelphia.

Morris was elected to the Pennsylvania legislature in October 1775 and to the Second Continental Congress the next month. For a long time, he opposed independence. Even by July 1776, after more than a year of war, he hoped the two sides would make up. But to prevent Pennsylvania from being the only colony to oppose independence, he and John Dickinson did not vote on July 2. This allowed Pennsylvania to slip into the independence column by a 3–2 vote.

Once independence was declared, Morris signed the document and devoted himself to the struggle. He reportedly vowed, "I pledge myself and all that I possess to the cause of my adopted country."

He kept his promise. Congress named him superintendent of finance, with the job of obtaining funds to pay for the war. Morris convinced rich people to lend money to the United States. He created the Bank of North America in Philadelphia—the country's first successful bank—which provided money for the cause. He also personally paid for supplies and soldiers' salaries. It was said that to help prepare for the pivotal Battle of Yorktown, he sacrificed more than a million dollars of his own money.

The British occupied Philadelphia in 1777–78, and Congress had to flee the city. Enemy troops invaded The Hills, partially wrecking the estate. Then, after the war, Morris made some bad land investments and ended up owing a great deal of money. At the time, people who owed money could be sent to prison. The

financial wizard who had spent his own fortune to win the war was sent to debtors' prison for three and a half years. Released in 1801 at the age of sixty-seven, he lived his last five years in poverty, consoled by the thought that he had helped build a nation. Morrisville, Pennsylvania, named in his honor, is one of the few reminders of the Financier of the Revolution.

BENJAMIN RUSH:
"All Will End Well"

Benjamin Rush

The leading American physician of the revolutionary era was also a statesman, college founder, antislavery leader, and signer of the Declaration of Independence.

Born near Philadelphia in early 1746, Benjamin Rush was just five when his father died. Ben's mother opened a grocery store in Philadelphia to support her seven children. A brilliant student, Ben entered Princeton College at thirteen and graduated just a year later.

A common way to become a doctor in colonial America was to serve as an apprentice to an established physician for a few years. Between the ages of fifteen and twenty, Rush worked as an apprentice under a Philadelphia physician. He showed so much promise that he was sent overseas to continue his medical education in Scotland.

After returning to Philadelphia in 1769, Dr. Rush treated mostly poor people at first, often for free. Over the years, he made many contributions to medicine. In 1786 he began the Philadelphia Dispensary, the country's first free medical clinic for the poor. For his work on behalf of the mentally ill, he became known as the Father of American Psychiatry. In addition, he helped establish veterinary medicine (medical treatment of animals) in America.

Rush was one of the first well-known Pennsylvanians to favor independence, but he was not yet in Congress when independence was declared. He, George Clymer, James Smith, George Ross, and George Taylor were the new delegates Pennsylvania sent to Congress on July 20 to sign the Declaration, along with four of the old delegates. Dr. Rush later described the signing that took place on August 2: "Awful silence pervaded the house when we were called up, one after another, to the table of the President of Congress to subscribe [sign] what was believed by many at that time to be our own death warrants."

Also in 1776, Rush married Julia Stockton, daughter of New Jersey signer

Richard Stockton. Benjamin and Julia Rush had thirteen children. During the war, Rush served as surgeon general in the Continental Army and was nearly captured by the British while tending the wounded.

For a while the outlook seemed so bleak that some Americans wanted George Washington dismissed as commander in chief. Dr. Rush expressed this view in a letter that was made public. Rush's reputation suffered as a result, for most Americans considered Washington's critics unpatriotic. Nevertheless, Dr. Rush felt confident about his country's cause, often using his favorite phrase to predict the war's outcome: "All will end well."

The war *did* end well, and afterward Rush kept working on behalf of his country. He helped found two Pennsylvania colleges, Dickinson College and Franklin and Marshall College. During the 1790s Rush was a leader in the fight to end slavery. From 1797 until his death, he served as treasurer of the U.S. Mint. Besides all this, he taught at the University of Pennsylvania, educating about 3,000 medical students in his lifetime. Dr. Benjamin Rush died in Philadelphia at the age of sixty-seven on April 19, 1813—the thirty-eighth anniversary of the first battle of the Revolution.

GEORGE CLYMER:

His "Dearest Wish" Was for Independence

ELEVEN YEARS after the Declaration of Independence was signed, American leaders created the nation's framework of government, the U.S. Constitution.

George Clymer was one of a small group of men who signed both documents.

Clymer was born in Philadelphia in 1739. His mother died when George was just a year old, and his father, a sea captain, died when the boy was seven. George was raised by his aunt and uncle.

George acquired his love of reading from the books in his aunt and uncle's large library. Following in his uncle's footsteps, he became a rich merchant. He also became a judge. But his "dearest wish," he once said, was for his country to become independent. Within days of the outbreak of war, Clymer was elected captain of a volunteer battalion that was called the Silk-Stockings because of their fancy uniforms.

Although Clymer did not fight in the war, through his business he helped supply the American army with gunpowder, which was needed to fire guns and cannons. He also helped supply flour and corn to feed the troops as well as tents for shelter.

Clymer was one of the five Pennsylvania signers who were sent to Congress sixteen days after the Declaration was approved. In late 1777 Congress asked Clymer to investigate conditions on the frontier. At Fort Pitt—now Pittsburgh, Pennsylvania—he made the first peace treaty between the Continental Congress and any Indian tribe. Unlike later American leaders, Clymer respected the Indians and by all accounts treated them fairly.

George and Elizabeth Meredith Clymer, whom he had married in 1765, had eight children, five of whom lived to adulthood. During the war the Clymers moved from place to place to avoid capture by the British. On one occasion, the British broke into their house and ransacked it not long after the Clymers had fled.

In 1787, George Clymer helped frame the U.S. Constitution. Besides Clymer, the only other signers of the Declaration who also signed the U.S. Constitution were Roger Sherman of Connecticut, George Read of Delaware, and Clymer's fellow Pennsylvanians Benjamin Franklin, Robert Morris, and James Wilson.

Clymer was also a trustee for the University of Pennsylvania. When it appeared that the university might have to close around 1797, he and other trustees took out personal loans to keep it going.

Having lived to see his "dearest wish" come true, George Clymer died in 1813 at the age of seventy-three. His friend Joseph Hopkinson, the son of New Jersey signer Francis Hopkinson, said of him, "His predominant passion was to promote every scheme for the improvement of his country."

JAMES WILSON:
"All Power Is Derived from the People"

James Wilson

Besides signing the Declaration of Independence, James Wilson played a key role in creating the U.S. Constitution and also served as one of the first Supreme Court justices. Despite all this, he ended his life "hunted like a wild beast," as he phrased it.

Born in Scotland in 1742, Wilson studied to become a minister but had to leave school due to his father's death. America was the land of opportunity for him, James decided. He came to New York in 1765 and soon settled in Philadelphia, where he taught Latin in the school that became the University of Pennsylvania.

A gifted writer and speaker, Wilson chose law as his life's work. By 1770 he had become a lawyer in Carlisle, Pennsylvania, about 100 miles west of Philadelphia. The next year he married Rachel Bird, with whom he had six children.

The young lawyer from Scotland sided strongly with his adopted country. In a pamphlet published in 1774, he declared that "all power is derived from the people." Since Americans had no representatives in the British Parliament, the Mother Country had no authority over the colonies. Wilson was elected to the Continental Congress in 1775, and served until 1777. The tall delegate with the thick glasses "spoke often in Congress," according to Benjamin Rush. Everyone listened closely, for, as Dr. Rush added, "His mind, while he spoke, was a blaze of light." Thanks to Wilson, Benjamin Franklin, and John Morton, Pennsylvania chose independence by a 3–2 vote on July 2, 1776.

Eleven years later, Wilson helped create the U.S. Constitution at the convention in Philadelphia. Many historians say that only James Madison of Virginia had more input to the Constitution than Wilson. One of the most democratic of the Constitution's forty signers, Wilson insisted that the government should serve the people and that the people should elect their lawmakers directly.

Wilson also spearheaded the drive for Pennsylvania to approve the Constitution, which it did on December 12, 1787, thereby becoming the second state, after only Delaware. Pennsylvania was nicknamed the Keystone State because, like the keystone in the center of an arch, it occupied a middle position among the thirteen new states.

President George Washington appointed James Wilson as one of the first justices of the U.S. Supreme Court in 1789. He served on the nation's highest court during his last years, which were often sad. His wife Rachel died in 1786. Seven years later Wilson married Hannah Gray, but their only child died in infancy. To make things worse, poor business decisions ruined him financially. Like Robert Morris, he was imprisoned for debt—first in New Jersey and then in North Carolina.

One of Wilson's last written comments was that he had been "hunted like a wild beast" by people attempting to collect money he owed. James Wilson, who had done so much for his country, died in poverty in North Carolina in 1798, less than a month shy of what would have been his fifty-sixth birthday.

JOHN MORTON:
"The Noble Cause of Liberty"

John Morton

A LITTLE-KNOWN PENNSYLVANIAN NAMED John Morton cast one of the most important votes in American history.

Morton was born near Philadelphia in what is now Delaware County, Pennsylvania, in 1724 or 1725. Of Swedish ancestry, John never knew his father, who died before his birth. When John was about seven, his mother remarried. John attended formal school for only about three months. Much of his later success was due to his stepfather, who taught him many subjects, including surveying and law.

John Morton grew up to become a farmer, surveyor, lawyer, and judge. He married Ann Justis, who like himself was of Swedish descent. John and Ann had five daughters and four sons.

Morton's political career began in 1756 with his election to the Pennsylvania legislature, where he served for about seventeen years. He was sent to the First Continental Congress in 1774, and to the Second Congress the following year. Although his section of Pennsylvania was home to many Loyalists, Morton favored independence. In a letter he sent to a friend in June 1775, Morton wrote that Pennsylvania would raise a large army "to support the Noble Cause of Liberty."

But as July 2, 1776, approached, John Morton was a troubled man. Should he vote for independence, which he personally favored, or should he vote against it, as many people in his home district urged him to do? Morton's decision would be of the utmost significance, for the Pennsylvania delegates were divided on the issue, and the colony could go either way.

Pennsylvania had seven delegates who would decide their colony's course on July 2. Thomas Willing and Charles Humphreys voted against independence. John Dickinson and Robert Morris did not vote. Benjamin Franklin and James Wilson voted for separation from England. John Morton followed his conscience, and by so doing pushed Pennsylvania onto the side of independence.

It was said that friends, neighbors, and even relatives turned against Morton because of his independence vote. By early 1777 he was very ill, perhaps with tuberculosis. In his last hours he made his own declaration to those who felt that he had let them down. He predicted that one day people would realize that voting for independence had been "the most glorious service I ever rendered my country." The first of the fifty-six signers to die, John Morton passed away at his birthplace on April 1, 1777, in his early fifties.

GEORGE ROSS:
Uncle to Betsy

Geo. Ross

ALTHOUGH HE WAS A SIGNER, George Ross is chiefly remembered today for his famous niece.

Born in Delaware in 1730, George studied law and moved to Lancaster, Pennsylvania, to practice. One of his first clients was Anne Lawler, a lovely young woman whom he married when he was twenty-one years old. George and Anne had a daughter and two sons.

George Ross was elected to Pennsylvania's colonial legislature in 1768. He opposed American independence for a long time. Many people accused him of siding with England as late as 1774. The next year he abruptly changed his views, perhaps convinced by the outbreak of war that English rule must end.

Ross was among the group elected to Congress on July 20, 1776. He took his seat on August 2 and signed the Declaration that very day.

George had a niece named Betsy Ross, who had a reputation in Philadelphia as an outstanding seamstress. According to a famous story, George Ross took George Washington and Robert Morris to visit Betsy in the summer of 1776. George Ross and his two companions asked Betsy to make a flag for the new nation, providing a rough idea of what they had in mind. Betsy Ross was said to have made at least one change in their plan. She thought that the flag's thirteen stars (which stood for the thirteen states) should be five-sided, not six-sided, as her uncle and his famous friends suggested. Betsy then made the first Stars and Stripes—or so it was said. Today, many historians credit Francis Hopkinson of New Jersey with designing the first Stars and Stripes. But even if she didn't help design or create the first Stars and Stripes, we do know that Betsy Ross made a number of flags for the young country.

During the war, George Ross helped make a treaty with the Indians and also served as a judge. He did not live to see his niece's flags fly over a victorious United States, however. Afflicted by severe gout like John Hancock, George Ross died in 1779, just three years after signing the Declaration of Independence.

GEORGE TAYLOR:

Mystery Man

Geo. Taylor

George Taylor of Pennsylvania is one of the two signers about whom the least is known. What a shame, for there are hints that Taylor had one of the most interesting lives of the fifty-six signers!

A minister's son, George was born in Ireland in 1716. As a young man he wanted to come to America but couldn't pay for his passage. George decided to join the thousands of other poor Europeans who sailed to America as indentured servants. These were people whose passage was paid by colonists already living in the new country. In return, indentured servants had to work without pay for about five years for the people who paid their way. Some indentured servants were treated almost like slaves, while others became more like family members of their masters.

George Taylor sailed to Pennsylvania around 1736, when he was about twenty years old. A Mr. Savage paid for his passage. At first George seems to have done physical labor in Mr. Savage's iron foundry outside Philadelphia. But when Mr. Savage learned that George had received some education, he promoted the young man to clerk. A few years later Mr. Savage died, and George married his widow, Anne Savage. George had two children with Anne. Now in charge of the ironworks, George had servants of his own. For years he carried on an affair with his housekeeper, Naomi Smith, and had five more children with her.

In 1764 Taylor was elected to the Pennsylvania legislature. Like the other two signers who were born in Ireland—his fellow Pennsylvanian James Smith and Matthew Thornton of New Hampshire—Taylor was a strong independence man. He had plenty of nerve, as demonstrated when he criticized the legendary Benjamin Franklin for not opposing Britain firmly enough at the start of the troubles. That was almost like criticizing George Washington. Part of Pennsylvania's new, more radical delegation elected to Congress in late July, Taylor signed the Declaration on or about August 2, 1776. Five months later, in January 1777, Congress sent him to make a treaty with Indians at Easton, Pennsylvania.

Soon after, Taylor left Congress and retired because of poor health. George Taylor, who had come to America as an indentured servant and had risen to sign the Declaration of Independence, died in February of 1781 at the age of about sixty-five. Had he lived another eight months, he would have seen the British surrender at Yorktown, Virginia.

JAMES SMITH:
Independence Was No Joke

Ja^s. Smith

IN 1805, A FIRE DESTROYED THE OFFICE AND PAPERS of James Smith, an elderly resident of York, Pennsylvania. Because documents that would have provided information about him went up in smoke, Smith is as obscure a figure as George Taylor.

Like Taylor, James Smith was born in Ireland. Most sources say he was born on the Emerald Isle in 1719, with a question mark after the date. But other dates of his birth, ranging from 1713 to 1722, have been given. Smith was something of a joker, so perhaps he enjoyed having people guess about his age. Around 1729, when James was perhaps ten years old (or maybe seven or sixteen), he sailed to America with his family. The Smiths settled in York County, Pennsylvania, which at that time was the backcountry. James attended school in Philadelphia and became a land surveyor and a lawyer. When he was about forty-one—give or take a few years—Smith married a Delaware woman named Eleanor Armor. The couple had five children.

A few years before the Revolutionary War, James Smith went into iron manufacturing. He lost a fortune in that business, but managed to make light of it. Smith admitted he had used poor judgment in placing the business in the hands of two assistants, "one [of whom] was a knave," he said, "and the other a fool."

One thing Smith didn't joke about was independence. He was so eager for it that in 1774 he raised what was believed to be Pennsylvania's first volunteer company of revolutionary militia. Along with Samuel Adams and Benjamin Franklin, he was one of the first people to call for a Continental Congress of American leaders. Elected to Congress on July 20, 1776, the patriot from Pennsylvania's backcountry signed the Declaration of Independence thirteen days later.

Few people today realize that for nine months between September 1777 and June 1778, the town of York, Pennsylvania, was the U.S. capital. Congress had abandoned Philadelphia because of the British invasion, and wouldn't return to that city until July 2, 1778. James Smith lived in York, so while Congress met there, his law office was used as the headquarters for the Board of War.

Smith left Congress in 1778. After brief stints in the Pennsylvania legislature and as a judge, he returned to the practice of law at the end of the war. He worked as a lawyer until about the age of eighty and was said to be the oldest attorney in the Keystone State. He died in York, Pennsylvania, on July 11, 1806, thirty years and one week after the adoption of the Declaration of Independence. At the time of his death, James Smith was at least eighty-four and perhaps as much as ninety-three years old.

IV. NEW JERSEY

Like several of its neighbors, New Jersey was part of New Sweden and New Netherland before the English took over. By 1663, however, only about 200 colonists lived in what became New Jersey.

A fleet of English warships arrived at New Netherland in 1664. The English took the region from the Dutch (people of the Netherlands) and gave English names to the former Dutch territory. New Jersey was named for England's Isle of Jersey. Its farms and gardens were so lovely that colonial New Jersey was called "the Garden of North America." Shipbuilding and fishing were important in New Jersey's seaside towns. New Jerseyans were also known for making glass and iron. By the mid-1770s New Jersey ranked ninth out of the thirteen colonies in population, with 125,000 colonists. But as the only colony with two colleges—Princeton and Rutgers—New Jersey was a leader in higher education.

In late 1774 New Jersey patriots burned British tea at what was called the Greenwich Tea Party. After the war began, New Jersey became known as the Cockpit of the Revolution because nearly 100 battles and skirmishes were fought there, including the important battles of Trenton, Princeton, and Monmouth.

The *Garden State*, as it would become known, had five signers of the Declaration of Independence. Because their state had such extensive fighting, the New Jersey signers suffered as much as or more than those from any other part of America.

NEW JERSEY

ame	Birth Date	Age at Signing	Marriage(s)	Children	Death Date	Age at Death
ichard Stockton	October 1, 1730	45	Annis Boudinot	6	February 28, 1781	50
rancis Hopkinson	October 2, 1737	38	Ann Borden	5	May 9, 1791	53
ohn Witherspoon	February 5, 1723	53	Elizabeth Montgomery Ann Dill	12	November 15, 1794	71
ohn Hart	Between 1708 and 1714	In his sixties	Deborah Scudder	13	May 11, 1779	Between 65 and 71
braham Clark	February 15, 1726	50	Sarah Hatfield	10	September 15, 1794	68

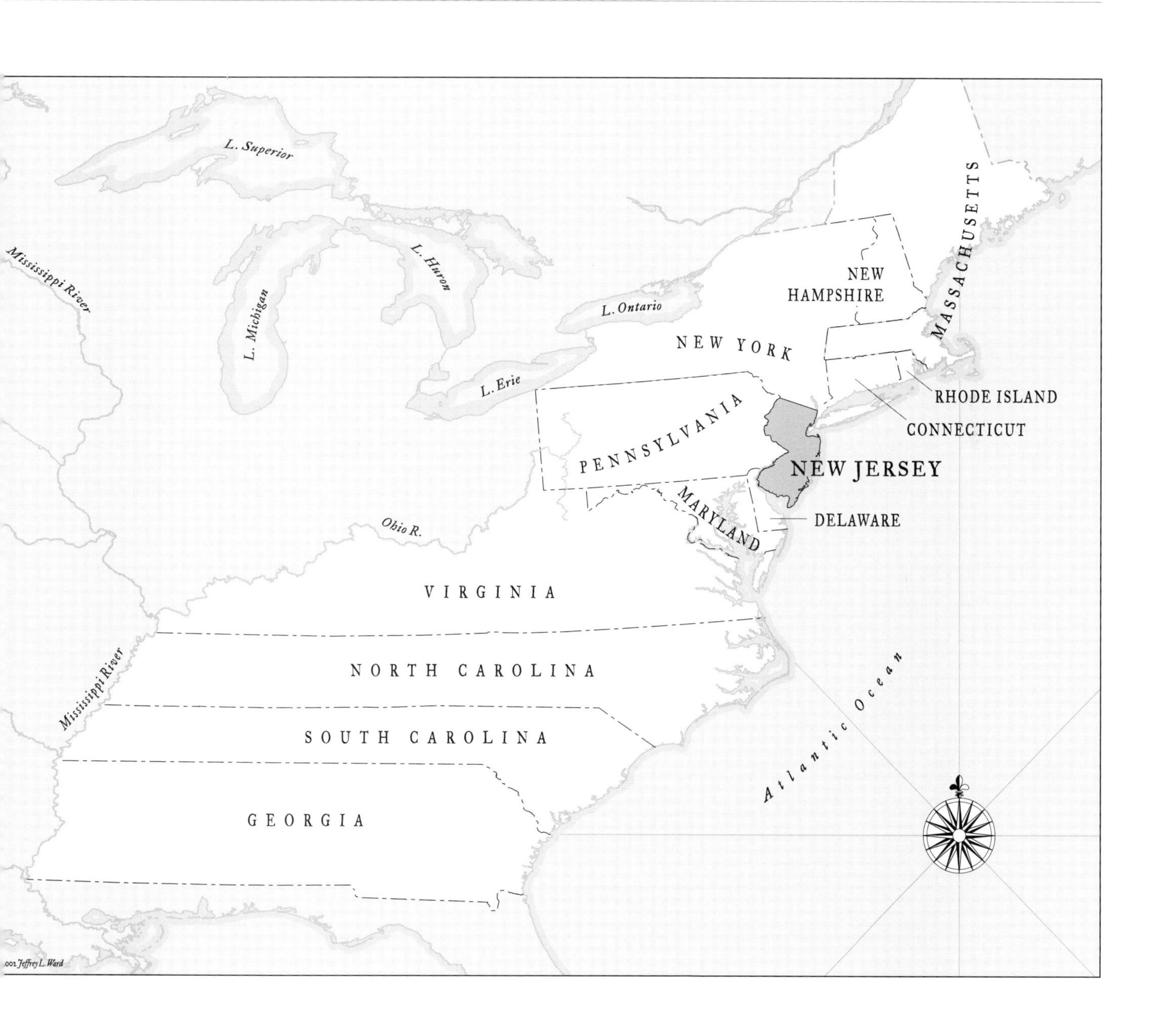

RICHARD STOCKTON:
Captured by the Enemy

Richd. Stockton

DURING REVOLUTIONARY TIMES New Jersey had many Loyalists—colonists who sided with Britain. In fact, most New Jerseyans may have still opposed independence as Congress prepared to vote on the issue in mid-1776. Pro-independence men took control of New Jersey's government, however. In June 1776 they arrested Benjamin Franklin's son William Franklin, who governed New Jersey for the king of England. New Jersey's revolutionary leaders also ousted their delegates to Congress who opposed independence. On June 22 they sent a new slate of delegates comprised of Richard Stockton, Abraham Clark, the Reverend John Witherspoon, Francis Hopkinson, and John Hart with orders to "declare the United Colonies independent" if they considered it proper.

Richard Stockton was born into a wealthy family in Princeton, New Jersey, in 1730. He grew up at Morven, his family's estate, and attended what is now Princeton University. A member of the college's first graduating class in 1748, Stockton became a lawyer. In 1755 he married Annis Boudinot, with whom he had six children.

New Jersey's royal government was good to Richard Stockton; he was a member of the council that advised the governor on important issues, as well as a New Jersey Supreme Court justice. By his forties he was a rich, successful man who spent much of his time breeding horses and collecting works of art at Morven.

When the troubles with England began, Stockton knew that he might lose everything, even his life, if he opposed the Mother Country. He was torn over what to do but in the end sided with America and was elected to represent his colony in Congress. Stockton and his fellow New Jersey delegates arrived just in time to hear the debate over independence. He voted for separation from England on July 2 and later signed his name to the Declaration: *Richd. Stockton.*

Congress appointed Stockton and George Clymer of Pennsylvania to visit the American army in New York. Stockton found that many of the men had worn out their shoes and were going barefoot. "There is not a single shoe or stocking to be had in this part of the world, or I would ride a hundred miles through the woods and purchase them with my own money," he reported.

By the time Stockton returned to Princeton, the British had overrun New Jersey, and George Washington's troops were retreating through the colony. Stockton fed and clothed as many of the American troops as he could. Then, with the British closing in, he fled with his wife and children to the home of a friend. Loyalists learned his whereabouts. One night in late 1776 a band of them surrounded the home, broke down the door, and pulled Richard Stockton out of bed. Stockton was roughed up and locked in jail. He was then sent to a New York prison. By the time he was released in 1777, his health was shattered and his home was destroyed.

During his last few years, Richard Stockton was so poor that he had to accept help from friends to support his family. He died in early 1781, before the war for which he had sacrificed so much was won. His home, Morven, was restored and became the official residence of New Jersey's governor from the 1950s until 1981.

FRANCIS HOPKINSON:
Mr. Stars and Stripes

Fra.s Hopkinson

MANY EXPERTS CREDIT a New Jersey signer with designing the U.S. flag.

Francis Hopkinson was born in Philadelphia in 1737. At the age of just fourteen, he was the first student to enroll in what turned into the University of Pennsylvania. Hopkinson became a lawyer, but for many years he did little legal work.

He was more interested in the arts. Francis drew pictures, wrote humorous poems, and composed songs. "My Days Have Been So Wondrous Free," which he wrote in 1759, was the first nonreligious song written by an American colonist.

For many years Francis had trouble earning a living. Around his thirtieth birthday he opened a store in Philadelphia, but it did poorly. Soon after, he married Ann Borden, granddaughter of the man for whom Bordentown, New Jersey, had been named. Francis and Ann, who would have five children, settled in Bordentown, where he turned back to law and became a successful attorney at the age of nearly forty.

In 1774 Hopkinson was appointed to serve on New Jersey governor William Franklin's council. His lofty position didn't influence his thinking: At the start of the conflict with England he declared his loyalty to America. In June 1776 he was elected to represent New Jersey in the Continental Congress, where he voted for and signed the Declaration. Congress also named him to head the Continental Navy Board and to serve as treasurer of loans.

During the war, Hopkinson lifted American spirits by writing songs, poems, and essays poking fun at the British. As head of the Navy Board, he organized a plan in which explosives were packed into kegs and floated down the Delaware River. No British ships were blown up, but American troops marched about singing "The Battle of the Kegs," Hopkinson's humorous song about the scheme.

The new country also needed a flag. Exactly how it originated has long been disputed. Francis Hopkinson claimed that he was the designer of the first Stars and Stripes, and nothing he ever did would lead us to think that he was lying. Perhaps both he and Betsy Ross were involved in the creation of the first U.S. flags. Hopkinson also designed the Great Seal of the State of New Jersey in 1776 as well as the seals of the cabinet departments of the U.S. government.

The British considered Hopkinson a prime enemy. When their troops entered Bordentown, they ransacked his home, but fortunately none of his family was injured.

One of Hopkinson's endearing traits was his affection for his friends. In a letter to Thomas Jefferson written in 1790, Francis closed by saying, "I have but few words to spare. If I had but six left, three of them would be spent in saying I love you." By then he had trouble writing because he had suffered a stroke. Francis Hopkinson died the next year at the age of only fifty-three.

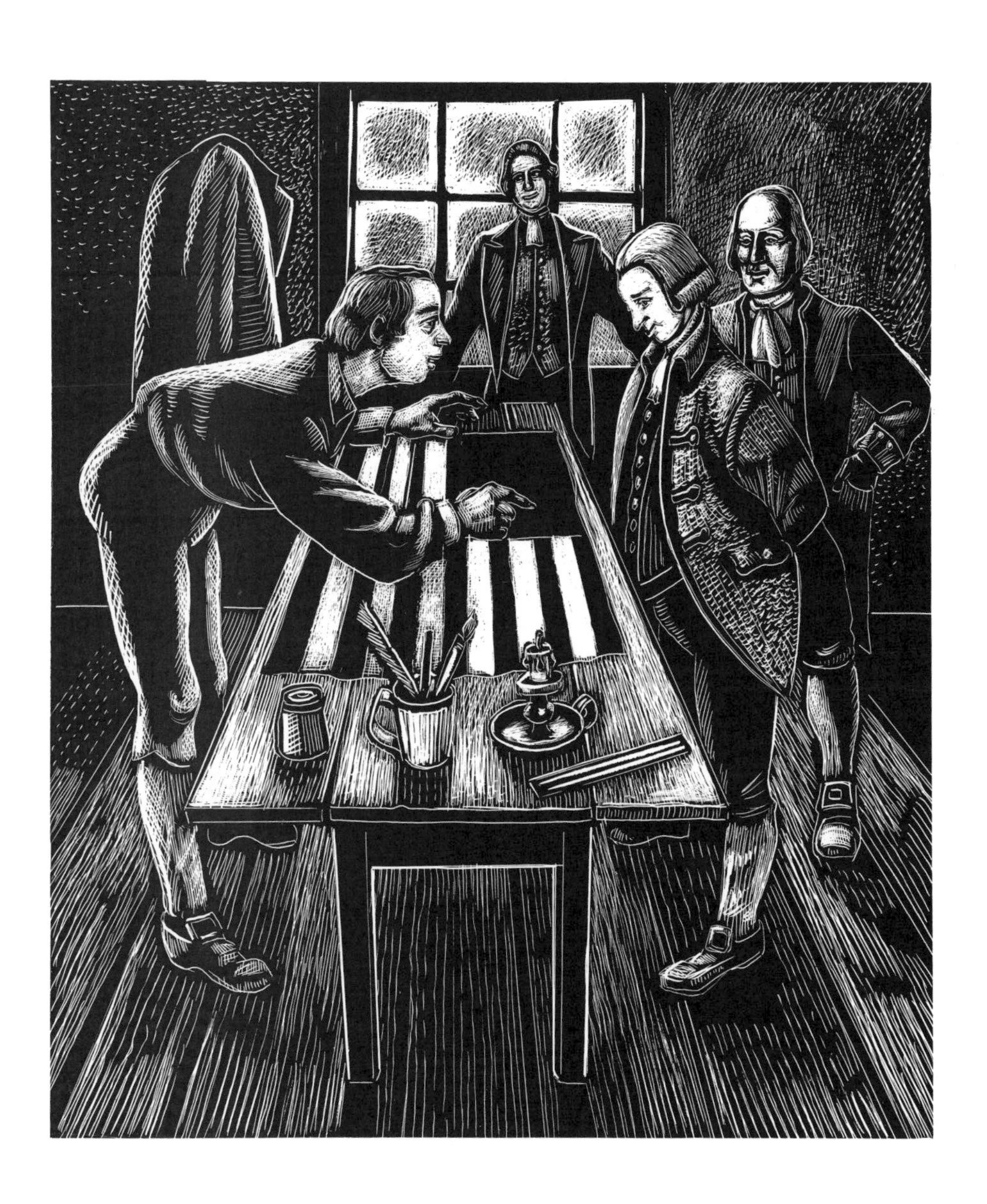

JOHN WITHERSPOON:

"Ripe for Independence"

A MINISTER FROM SCOTLAND was one of the leaders in America's drive for independence.

John Witherspoon was born near Edinburgh into a family of clergymen in 1723. By age four John could read the Bible. He entered college at thirteen, and at twenty he was licensed to preach.

In 1746 the young minister helped raise troops to fight Scottish Highlanders who were rebelling against English domination. The rebels captured him, imprisoned him in a castle, and threatened to kill him. He was released a few days later, but afterward he had trouble sleeping, and he would sometimes faint in the middle of a sermon.

Nonetheless, he became one of Scotland's leading Presbyterian ministers. Princeton College in New Jersey asked him to become its president. However, his wife Elizabeth, with whom he had ten children, didn't want to leave Scotland. Finally Benjamin Rush, a young Princeton graduate studying in Scotland, convinced Mrs. Witherspoon to cross the ocean. The Witherspoons sailed to America in the spring of 1768. For twenty-six years the Reverend John Witherspoon served as Princeton's president, helping to make it a great institution and sometimes paying the tuition of poorer students out of his own pocket.

John Witherspoon loved his new home, claiming that he had "become an American the moment he landed." He sided with America against England and also tried to turn his students against the Mother Country. Elected to Congress in June 1776, he arrived in time to hear a delegate say on July 2 that America wasn't yet ripe for independence. "It is not only ripe for the measure," declared Witherspoon, "but in danger of rotting for the want of it!" Congress voted for independence that day, and Witherspoon became the only clergyman to sign the Declaration.

For most of the period between mid-1776 and late 1782, Witherspoon represented New Jersey in Congress, serving on more than 100 committees. To remind people that he believed God was on America's side, he always wore his minister's clothes to Congress. Even when America's prospects looked bleak, Witherspoon remained a beacon of hope, despite his personal sufferings. In 1777 John and Elizabeth's son James was killed at the Battle of Germantown in what is now Philadelphia. The British wrecked the Witherspoon farm near Princeton, and part of the Battle of Princeton in 1777 was fought right on the college campus. The college was damaged so extensively that it had to close for a time.

John Witherspoon spent his last years working to rebuild the college. He was also a member of the New Jersey convention that approved the U.S. Constitution on December 18, 1787, transforming New Jersey into our third state.

Elizabeth Witherspoon died in 1789. Two years later, the sixty-eight-year-old minister married twenty-four-year-old Ann Dill, with whom he had two daughters. Unfortunately, he became blind around the time that he married Ann and couldn't see anything for his last three years. The Reverend John Witherspoon, who had crossed an ocean to help America win its independence, died on his farm near Princeton in 1794 at the age of seventy-one.

"HONEST JOHN" HART:
Fugitive Signer

John Hart

LONG BEFORE "HONEST ABE" LINCOLN, there was a New Jersey farmer known as "Honest John" Hart. He lived in obscurity for about sixty-five years, then stepped into the limelight for a few months toward the end of his life.

No one is sure when Hart was born. Various sources say 1708, 1711, or 1714. It is not clear where he was born, either. Some say Connecticut, while others claim it was Hopewell, New Jersey, an area where he lived most of his life. In 1739 he bought a farm and married a neighbor named Deborah Scudder. The couple had thirteen children and with hard work became rather well-to-do.

Called "Honest John" by his neighbors because of his integrity and fairness, Hart served many years as a judge and colonial legislator. He was among the five men chosen as New Jersey's fresh slate of congressional delegates on June 22, 1776. Hart took his seat on July 1, voted for independence the next day, and signed the Declaration on August 2. Soon after, he returned to New Jersey to help transform it into a state.

But because he had signed the Declaration, Hart's troubles were just starting. The British offered a reward for his capture. When the enemy advanced near Hopewell in late 1776, Hart rode home to his family. Deborah, who was very ill at the time, begged her husband to take the children who were still living at home and hide. John placed the children with relatives, then fled, barely escaping capture by enemy troops. For days John Hart, who was about sixty-five years old, hid in the woods and hills. He slept in caves or out in the open in the frigid December weather. British officials offered to pardon him if he would surrender and give up the patriot cause, but he refused. Hart couldn't return home until after George Washington's troops had won the Battle of Princeton on January 3, 1777. He found that his wife had died and his home was in ruins.

John Hart was never able to gather his children back together. His health wrecked by his days as a fugitive, he died in May 1779. Dr. Benjamin Rush wrote about "Honest John" Hart: "A plain, honest, well-meaning Jersey farmer, with little education, but with good sense and virtue enough to pursue the true interests of his country."

ABRAHAM CLARK:

"In the Darkest Hours"

MOST OF THE SIGNERS WERE rich, well-educated, and influential men. Abraham Clark may have been the signer who was closest to being a typical citizen.

He was born in what is now Elizabeth, New Jersey, on the day after Valentine's Day of 1726. His father was a farmer, but Abraham was too frail and sickly to do farm work. He became a surveyor—a person who determines land boundaries. And although he never became an official lawyer, he studied law on his own and did a great deal of legal work for his neighbors. He was referred to as "the poor man's lawyer" because he often worked for free or for small fees. Around 1749 Abraham married Sarah Hatfield, with whom he had ten children.

Clark became very popular with poorer New Jerseyans. Like them, he disliked the "bigwigs"—the rich and powerful people who controlled most affairs in colonial America. Clark himself didn't wear a wig, big *or* small. Pictures of him show a plain-looking man with a striking resemblance to Connecticut signer Roger Sherman.

From 1752 to 1766 Clark served as clerk of the New Jersey colonial legislature. Next he became county sheriff. When the struggle with Britain began, no one doubted which side Clark would take. One of five new radical delegates New Jersey sent to Congress in June, Clark wrote home about the Declaration on July 4, 1776: "We can die but once. . . . It is gone so far that we must now be a free independent State or a Conquered Country."

Few signers suffered as much as Abraham Clark. The British destroyed all of his property. Furthermore, one of his sons was captured by the British and held on a prison ship. It was said that the British offered to release his son if Clark abandoned the American cause, but that, like "Honest John" Hart, he refused to betray his country.

After the war, Clark was elected to the U.S. Congress. An event in Congress demonstrated Clark's lifelong struggle on behalf of the average citizen. Some bigwigs wanted the nation's coins to show a picture of whoever happened to be president. Clark preferred that our coins display the word *Liberty* along with designs emblematic of our nation. Congress voted to follow Clark's method, and today all U.S. coins have the word *Liberty* on them.

The man who fought for liberty much of his life died in 1794 at the age of sixty-eight. The people of New Jersey inscribed these words on his tombstone:

HE LOVED HIS COUNTRY,
AND ADHERED TO HER CAUSE,
IN THE DARKEST HOURS OF HER STRUGGLES
AGAINST OPPRESSION

V. DELAWARE

Soldiers sent by Sweden came to what is now Delaware in 1638 and built a fort at present-day Wilmington. It was Delaware's first permanent colonial settlement as well as the first in New Sweden, which would extend into Pennsylvania and New Jersey. Under Swedish rule, settlers in Delaware built America's first log cabins. Then, in 1655, the Dutch captured New Sweden and made Delaware part of their New Netherland territory. By the early 1660s, what is now Delaware had only about 1,000 settlers, however.

With their conquest of New Netherland in 1664, the English took control of Delaware, which they named for Lord De La Warr, a governor of Virginia. At first part of Pennsylvania, Delaware was finally granted its own colonial legislature in 1704. Most Delaware colonists grew corn and wheat and raised chickens, cows, and pigs on small farms. By 1775 Delaware had roughly 40,000 colonists and was tied with Georgia as the least populous of England's thirteen colonies.

The most famous event in Delaware history occurred when Caesar Rodney tried to reach Philadelphia in time for his colony to choose independence. In the end, the Declaration was signed not only by Rodney and Thomas McKean but also by George Read, who had opposed independence. On September 3, 1777, the U.S. flag was reportedly flown for the very first time at the Battle of Cooch's Bridge in Delaware.

A decade later, on December 7, 1787, Delaware approved the U.S. Constitution, becoming the first colony to achieve statehood under the new national government. It has been called the First State ever since.

DELAWARE

Name	*Birth Date*	*Age at Signing*	*Marriage(s)*	*Children*	*Death Date*	*Age at Death*
Thomas McKean	March 19, 1734	About 42	Mary Borden Sarah Armitage	11	June 24, 1817	83
Caesar Rodney	October 7, 1728	47	Never married	0	June 1784	55
George Read	September 18, 1733	42	Gertrude Ross Till	5	September 21, 1798	65

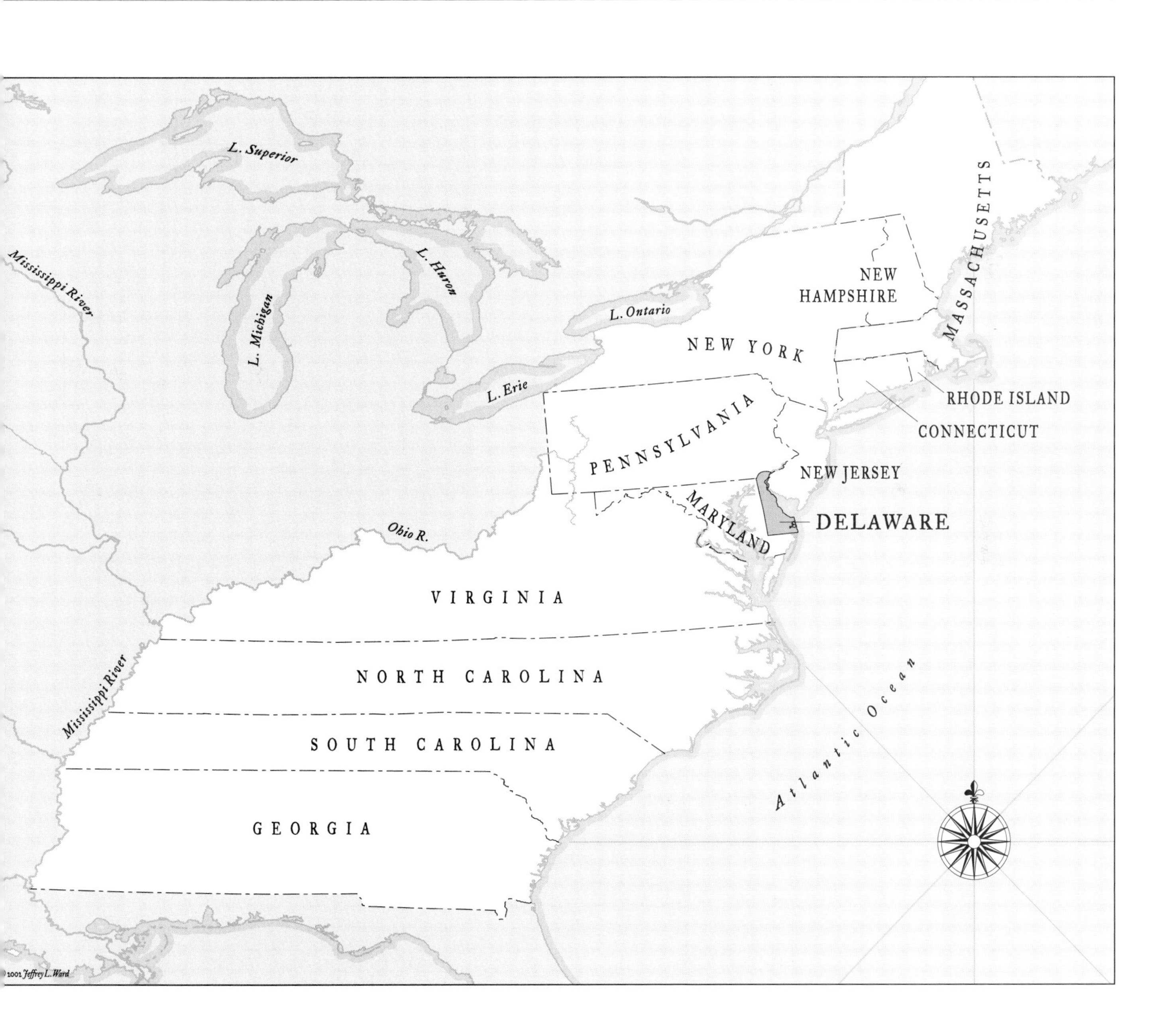

THOMAS MCKEAN:
The Man Who Got Things Done

A Delaware signer held more major offices than any other American of his time—perhaps more than any other American ever.

Thomas McKean (pronounced *McKane*) was born in Pennsylvania in 1734, of Scotch-Irish heritage. By age eight Thomas was learning Latin and Greek in school. He later studied law with a cousin, and at twenty he became an attorney. By then he was over six feet in height, making him a giant in an age when the average man stood about five feet, six inches tall.

In 1763 he married Mary Borden, sister of Francis Hopkinson's wife Ann. Thomas and Mary had six children. After she died in 1773, he married Sarah Armitage, with whom he had five more children.

McKean practiced law and lived at various times in Philadelphia, Pennsylvania, and nearby Delaware. Although serious by nature, he sometimes used humor to sway juries, as in the case of a client accused of saying things that damaged a neighbor's reputation. McKean called witnesses who testified that his client was a known liar. The man was so notorious a liar, argued McKean, that no one could have believed his comments about the neighbor. The jury laughed and found McKean's client not guilty of slander.

Among the posts he held in Delaware, McKean served in the legislature for more than fifteen years. At the time, Delaware's laws were written in scattered places. In 1762 McKean and fellow legislator Caesar Rodney were asked to collect, revise, and publish all of Delaware's laws. The pair produced a two-volume set of laws by the following year.

After the struggle with England began, a British sympathizer called him "the violent raging rebel McKean" because he supported his country so fiercely. For nearly ten years starting in 1774 McKean represented Delaware in Congress. On July 1, 1776—the day before the official vote on independence—McKean learned something shocking. George Read, who had been expected to vote for independence, was actually going to vote against it. McKean dispatched a messenger, imploring Caesar Rodney to hurry to Philadelphia.

Before he could sign the Declaration, McKean went off to fight in the American army. He led troops in New Jersey and was nearly killed in action. "About twenty Cannon Balls flew close to me sometimes on one side and sometimes on the other and some just over my head," he wrote to his wife. He later returned to Congress, where he signed the Declaration, probably sometime in 1777.

McKean held so many posts during and after the war that people must have thought he had a twin. From 1777 to 1799 he was chief justice of Pennsylvania. While holding that office, he served as governor of Delaware in 1777. In 1781 he was briefly president of the Continental Congress. Later, from 1799 to 1808, he was governor of Pennsylvania. In addition, he helped frame state constitutions for both Delaware and Pennsylvania.

The man who got things done died at age eighty-three in 1817. Always a person who did things in a big way, Thomas McKean left behind *thirty-four* grandchildren.

CAESAR RODNEY:
He Rode All Night

NO SIGNER SHOWED GREATER COURAGE than Caesar Rodney.

Born near Dover, Delaware, in 1728, Caesar attended school briefly but was taught at home by his mother. His father died when Caesar was seventeen, so he took over the family farm and helped his mother raise his six younger sisters and brothers. His child-raising finally ended in his late twenties, and he could choose a career. Thanks to an inheritance from his father, money was no problem. Caesar decided to devote his life to public service.

In 1755 he was chosen sheriff of Delaware's Kent County. Over the next twenty years he served his colony in many ways. He was clerk of the orphans' court and elected to Delaware's legislature. Caesar Rodney was so highly respected that he was appointed to Delaware's Supreme Court—even though he hadn't studied law!

Despite his success under the colonial government, Rodney sided with America against England. Delawareans chose him to represent them in the Continental Congress. After meeting him at the First Congress in September 1774, John Adams wrote in his diary: "Caesar Rodney is the oddest looking Man in the World. He is tall, thin and slender as a Reed, [and] pale. His face is not bigger than a large Apple, Yet there is Sense and Fire, Spirit, Wit, and Humor in his [expression]."

His odd appearance resulted from poor health. Asthma often made his breathing difficult. Gout sometimes left him unable to walk. But his biggest problem was cancer. In 1768 part of a tumor had been removed from his face, leaving a deep gash across his cheek that he covered with a green silk scarf.

Unfortunately, the operation had not rid him of cancer. His best chance for a cure, it was believed, was to seek treatment in England, But a revolutionary leader couldn't go to a country that might "cure" him by removing his head. So, by siding with America, Caesar Rodney may have given up his chance to conquer his disease, which steadily grew worse.

On the eve of the independence vote, Rodney was in Delaware, where he had been called upon to oppose a threatened Loyalist uprising. Caesar was feeling ill. Heavy rain was falling. But immediately upon learning from Thomas McKean's messenger that he was needed in Congress, he set out in a desperate attempt to reach Philadelphia in less than a day. According to tradition, he rode the entire eighty miles on horseback, galloping along muddy roads and crossing swollen streams. Modern historians say that he probably traveled at least part of the way by carriage. In any event, after fourteen hours of travel he reached Philadelphia in time to tip Delaware into the independence column, two votes to one.

Rodney recruited many Delaware men to serve in the American forces, and even fought in the army himself for a time. From the spring of 1778 to late 1781 he was Delaware's governor. He lived long enough to enjoy the victory, dying in June 1784—less than a year after the final peace treaty was signed ending the Revolution.

Caesar Rodney never married. His brother Thomas, whom he had helped raise, became a Delaware lawmaker and judge. Caesar also helped raise Thomas's son, Caesar Augustus Rodney, who served as attorney general of the United States from 1807 to 1811.

GEORGE READ:
He Signed, Signed, Signed

Geo Read

Not only was George Read one of six men to sign both the Declaration of Independence and the U.S. Constitution, he signed one of these documents twice.

Born in Maryland in 1733, George began studying with a Philadelphia attorney when he was about fifteen. He became a lawyer and moved to New Castle, Delaware. Thinking it might hamper his career, George decided not to marry, but a fellow lawyer, George Ross, had a sister who caught Read's eye. George Read and Gertrude Ross Till married and over the years had five children. The two brothers-in-law named George—Read and Ross—would both later sign the Declaration of Independence.

In 1765 Read was elected to Delaware's legislature, where he was a leading opponent of British taxes. He was sent to the Continental Congress in 1774, and served there until 1777. First and foremost, he wanted what was best for Delaware. Convinced that most Delawareans weren't ready to separate from England, he voted against independence on July 2, 1776. Yet once independence was declared, Read thought it best for Delaware to unite with the rest of the country, so he shifted gears and signed the Declaration.

In the fall of 1777, the British captured Wilmington, Delaware, seizing the first governor of the state, John McKinly. Needed in Delaware to take over as governor, Read left Philadelphia with his family and took a roundabout route home to avoid the enemy. While crossing the Delaware River, the Reads were captured by British troops on an armed barge. Had they known George Read's identity, the British would have imprisoned him, but he convinced them that he was a local man traveling with his family. The British helped the Reads to dry ground, unaware that they had let a signer slip through their fingers.

George Read served as Delaware's governor from November 1777 to March

1778. Governor Read worked to raise troops and supplies for American forces during one of the most difficult periods of the war.

He was a leading spokesman for the rights of the small states at the Constitutional Convention in Philadelphia in 1787. Another delegate, John Dickinson, had to leave the convention early because of illness and authorized George Read to sign the document for him. As a result, Read signed the Constitution twice—once for himself and once in place of Dickinson. Read was also instrumental in convincing Delaware's leaders to quickly approve the Constitution. Thanks largely to his efforts, Delaware became the First State by approving the Constitution on December 7, 1787.

From 1789 to 1793 George Read served as one of his state's first U.S. senators. He resigned his Senate seat in 1793 to become chief justice of the Delaware Supreme Court, a post he held until his death in 1798, three days after his sixty-fifth birthday.

VI. RHODE ISLAND

Rhode Island—the tiniest of the fifty states—was the smallest of the thirteen colonies. However, in one way "Little Rhody" was a giant.

Many people came to America seeking religious freedom. Yet once in America, some of them persecuted their neighbors in turn for their religious beliefs. Rhode Island was settled by people who were forced out of Massachusetts for religious reasons.

Massachusetts officials decided to ship Roger Williams, a minister who believed in freedom of worship, back to England. Williams fled through the wilderness to Rhode Island. In 1636 he and some followers founded Providence, Rhode Island's first colonial town and the first American town to offer complete freedom of religion. Other people who came to Rhode Island seeking religious liberty included Anne Hutchinson, who helped found Portsmouth in 1638. Because it welcomed people of various faiths, Rhode Island is honored today as the birthplace of religious freedom in America.

By the start of the Revolutionary War, Rhode Island was home to about 55,000 colonists—less than every other colony except Georgia and Delaware. The Rhode Island colonists farmed, built ships, and worked as merchants.

The smallest colony had the fewest signers. William Ellery and Stephen Hopkins signed the Declaration of Independence for Rhode Island. With twenty-three children between them, Ellery and Hopkins also helped populate the Ocean State, as Rhode Island became known.

RHODE ISLAND

ame	Birth Date	Age at Signing	Marriage(s)	Children	Death Date	Age at Death
ILLIAM ELLERY	December 22, 1727	48	Ann Remington Abigail Carey	16	February 15, 1820	92
EPHEN HOPKINS	March 7, 1707	69	Sarah Scott Anne Smith	7	July 13, 1785	78

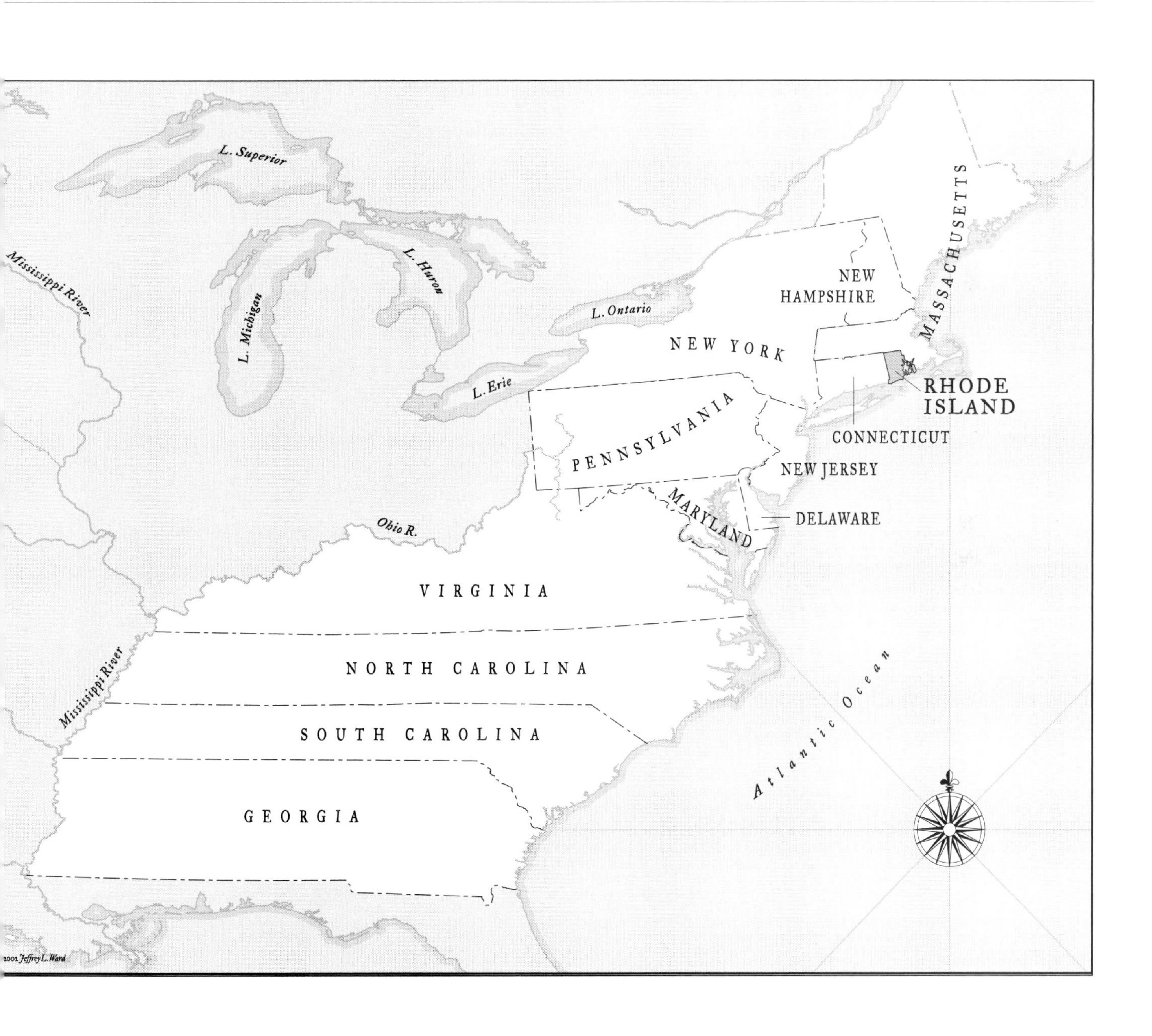

WILLIAM ELLERY:

"Undaunted Resolution"

William Ellery

BECAUSE OF STORIES HE TOLD his grandchildren, William Ellery is at the center of a great mystery about the signing of the Declaration.

Born in Newport, Rhode Island, in 1727, Ellery graduated from Harvard and then married Ann Remington. He wanted to become an attorney, but in colonial times law didn't necessarily provide a steady income. William and Ann Ellery had six children. After Ann died in 1764, William married Abigail Carey, with whom he had ten more children. With sixteen sons and daughters, William Ellery needed a reliable income, so despite his dislike for the business world he worked as a merchant for twenty years. Finally, at age forty, he had enough money to pursue his dream. He began studying law, and in 1769 the forty-two-year-old William Ellery at long last went to work as an attorney.

Barely five feet tall, chubby, balding, and nearsighted, Ellery was known as a gentle and kindly man. He loved to garden, spending much of his free time growing flowers and vegetables. But when the British began taxing the Americans, Ellery became one of Newport's "High Sons of Liberty"—a term describing the most rebellious Americans. In March 1776 Samuel Ward, a Rhode Island delegate to the Continental Congress, died of smallpox. Ellery was chosen to replace him, and that May he journeyed to Philadelphia to join the little colony's other delegate, Stephen Hopkins. Ellery probably made most of the 250-mile trip on horseback. Instead of traveling by carriage like many other important lawmakers, he rode nearly everywhere, earning him the nickname "the Congressman on Horseback."

Ellery joined Congress in time to support and sign the Declaration. The British didn't forget it. After seizing Newport in December 1776, they burned the Ellery family's home and destroyed much of the town. Ellery later had to borrow money from his friends to pay his expenses.

William Ellery served in Congress on and off until 1785. One of his last deeds in Congress was an unsuccessful effort to end slavery in the country.

The "Congressman on Horseback" lived to ninety-two—an older age than any other signer except Maryland's Charles Carroll and perhaps Pennsylvania's James Smith. In his later years, Ellery sometimes told his grandchildren about the signing. He had taken a seat near the Declaration to watch all the delegates sign one by one, and each man showed "undaunted resolution" as he signed, Ellery claimed.

The mystery is, we know of no ceremony like the one Ellery described, when all members of Congress signed the Declaration on the same day. Perhaps Ellery exaggerated the events of August 2, 1776, when most but not all of the fifty-six signers put their John Hancocks on the document. There is another intriguing possibility. Some people believe there really *was* a mass signing of the Declaration on July 4, on a copy of the document that has been lost. If that occurred, it may have been the event Ellery remembered and described to his grandchildren.

STEPHEN HOPKINS:

"Liberty Is the Greatest Blessing"

Step. Hopkins

BESIDES LEADING HIS COLONY to independence, Stephen Hopkins improved life in Rhode Island in many ways.

Born in Providence in 1707, Hopkins grew up in what is now Scituate, Rhode Island. His mother was a member of the Religious Society of Friends (commonly called the Quakers), a faith that despised war and opposed slavery. For much of his life, Stephen was a Quaker too, adopting their plain dress and many of their beliefs.

Stephen never attended school, but learned to read and write from his mother. When he wasn't working on his family's farm, he read about history and law. At nineteen he married Sarah Scott, with whom he had seven children. Following her death he married a widow named Anne Smith, but they had no children together.

At the tender age of twenty-five, Hopkins was chosen as Scituate's town clerk. He rose to become governor of Rhode Island as well as its Supreme Court chief justice. In addition, Hopkins founded a patriot newspaper, the *Providence Gazette,* and served as the first chancellor of what is now Brown University.

In 1764 Hopkins wrote a pamphlet called *The Rights of Colonies Examined.* "Liberty is the greatest blessing that men enjoy," asserted Hopkins, who went on to say that Britain couldn't govern the thirteen colonies without the Americans' consent. These were bold words—especially since they came from a colonial governor. The pamphlet was reprinted in newspapers across America and helped make Hopkins a national figure.

While serving as chief justice in 1772, Hopkins became involved in one of the events that sparked the Revolutionary War. A group of Americans burned the British ship *Gaspee* off the Rhode Island shore and shot a British officer. Everyone knew who the culprits were, but instead of punishing them, Hopkins did all he could to make sure they weren't caught. The British hated him for this, but to the American patriots he was a hero.

In June 1774 Rhode Island became the first of the thirteen colonies to elect delegates to the First Continental Congress. Stephen Hopkins and Samuel Ward were chosen. While many other delegates hoped to make peace, Hopkins warned that Americans would have to fight for their liberty: "Powder and ball [meaning gunpowder and bullets] will decide this question. The gun and bayonet alone will finish the contest in which we are engaged, and any of you who cannot bring your minds to this mode of adjusting the question had better retire."

The firebrand from the smallest colony made another famous comment when signing the Declaration in 1776. At sixty-nine the oldest of the fifty-six signers except for Benjamin Franklin, Hopkins suffered from a condition that caused him to tremble, and he had to guide his right hand with his left hand as he signed. Wanting everyone to know that he wasn't shaking from fear, as he signed, he said, "My hand trembles but my heart does not!"

Hopkins was instrumental in creating the Continental Navy—now the U.S. Navy—which his brother Esek Hopkins commanded. Also thanks to his efforts, in 1774 Rhode Island became the first colony to outlaw the importing of slaves. Stephen Hopkins died at his home in Providence in 1785 at the age of seventy-eight.

VII. CONNECTICUT

The first known explorer in Connecticut, Adriaen Block of the Netherlands, sailed up what the Indians called Quinnehtukqut, or "Long River," in 1614. The Dutch built a fort and trading post where Hartford now stands in 1633 but failed to settle the area.

English people from Massachusetts were the region's first colonists. They founded Connecticut's first colonial town, Windsor, in 1633, and began Hartford in 1635. English colonists spelled the river's name *Connecticut* and gave that name to the colony.

Connecticut families grew corn, apples, and peas. The colony was also an early manufacturing center. During the mid-1700s, America's first tinware and factory-made hats were produced there. Other goods from nails to clocks were made in Connecticut. With 200,000 settlers by the eve of the Revolution, Connecticut was just average in population, but it had two of the thirteen colonies' larger cities. New Haven, home to Yale College, had nearly 10,000 people and was America's sixth-largest city. Norwich ranked seventh, with over 7,000 colonists.

Known in colonial days as the Land of Steady Habits and later as the Constitution State, Connecticut had four signers. Samuel Huntington and Oliver Wolcott later governed the state. Roger Sherman became a U.S. senator. And William Williams helped Connecticut approve the U.S. Constitution. Connecticut also produced Nathan Hale, who was captured by the British while working as a spy for George Washington. Before he was hanged, the young teacher said the famous words, "I only regret that I have but one life to lose for my country."

CONNECTICUT

Name	*Birth Date*	*Age at Signing*	*Marriage(s)*	*Children*	*Death Date*	*Age at Death*
Oliver Wolcott	November 20, 1726	49	Laura Collins	5	December 1, 1797	71
Samuel Huntington	July 3, 1731	45	Martha Devotion	0	January 5, 1796	64
William Williams	March 18, 1731	45	Mary Trumbull	3	August 2, 1811	80
Roger Sherman	April 19, 1721	55	Elizabeth Hartwell Rebecca Prescott	15	July 23, 1793	72

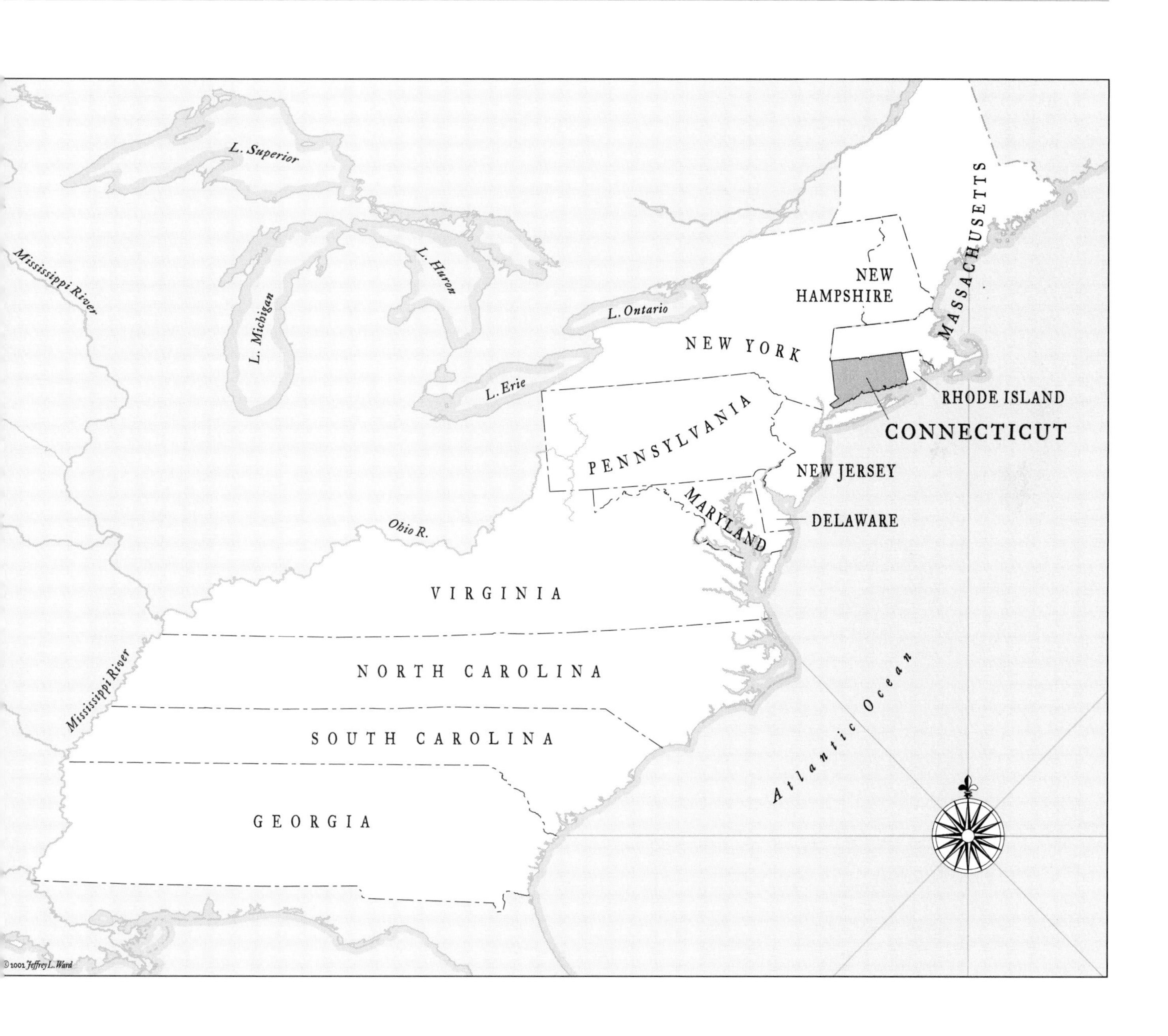

OLIVER WOLCOTT:
The Man with the Headless Statue

Oliver Wolcott

A Connecticut signer is best remembered for what he did with a statue of the king of England.

Oliver Wolcott, the son of a governor of the Connecticut Colony, was born in what is now East Windsor, Connecticut, in 1726. After graduating from Yale at twenty, Oliver did a variety of things. Like many other colonists, he served as a soldier on England's side when the Mother Country fought France for control of North America. In 1751 he moved to Litchfield, Connecticut, where he worked as a merchant and became the county sheriff. In his late twenties he married Laura Collins, with whom he had five children.

Wolcott was elected to the Connecticut legislature in 1764, and to the Continental Congress in the fall of 1775. He was a powerful voice for separation from England, but illness forced him to leave Congress in late June 1776, a few days before the vote on independence.

While returning to Connecticut, Wolcott passed through New York City, where George Washington ordered the Declaration of Independence read to his troops on July 9. That night New York patriots, excited by the separation from England, pulled down a statue of Great Britain's king George III. The statue's head came off and was later shipped to England. Oliver Wolcott placed the pieces of the headless statue into wagons and took them home to Litchfield with him. There the statue was melted. According to a count someone kept, the two Wolcott daughters and their friends shaped the metal into more than 42,000 bullets. American soldiers later fired the bullets at English troops.

Wolcott returned to Congress in October 1776, and then or perhaps even later signed the Declaration. Meanwhile, because of his earlier experience as a soldier, he was made a general and placed in command of Connecticut troops. He helped defeat the British at the Battle of Saratoga in New York in the fall of

1777. Reportedly some of the bullets made from the statue of the king were used in this battle.

Later in life, Wolcott served as Connecticut's state governor from 1796 until his death in late 1797 at age seventy-one. Oliver and Laura's son, Oliver Wolcott Jr., was the nation's secretary of the treasury from 1795 to 1800.

SAMUEL HUNTINGTON:
"I Shall Always Love My Country"

Sam^el Huntington

Some historians consider Samuel Huntington the first president of the United States.

Huntington was born in Windham, Connecticut, on July 3, 1731. At about sixteen, he was apprenticed to a cooper (a maker of barrels and other wooden containers). Samuel studied law books in his spare time, and at twenty-two he passed the test to practice law in Connecticut. A few years later he moved to Norwich, Connecticut, where he married Martha Devotion, a minister's daughter.

A shy, quiet man who wasn't much of a speaker or writer, Samuel Huntington won the respect of Connecticut people for his fairness and hard work. At thirty-three he was elected to the Connecticut legislature, and at forty-one he was made a judge. In the fall of 1775 he was elected to the Continental Congress, and he took his seat early the next year.

In a letter to George Washington, Huntington once wrote, "I shall always love my Country." On the day before his forty-fifth birthday he voted for independence, and later he signed the Declaration for his state.

John Jay of New York, the president of the Continental Congress, was appointed U.S. minister to Spain in September 1779. Congress elected steady, reliable Samuel Huntington as the new president. Huntington held the highest position in the national government from September 1779 to July 1781. Because he was president of Congress when the nation's first framework of government, the Articles of Confederation, took effect on March 1, 1781, Huntington has been called the first real president of the United States. But of course most people reserve that honor for George Washington, who was elected president under our present governmental framework, the U.S. Constitution.

Samuel Huntington later served as Connecticut's third state governor for ten years, from 1786 to 1796. He was still governor when he died at the age of sixty-four. Among his honors, the town of Huntington, Indiana, was named for him.

Although they had no children of their own, Samuel and Martha raised their nephew and niece, Samuel and Frances. Samuel Huntington, the nephew, was governor of the state of Ohio from 1808 to 1810.

WILLIAM WILLIAMS:

"A Cause Unspeakably Important"

THE PEOPLE IN THE *Land of Steady Habits* had a reputation for sticking to their job—often for decades. No patriot exemplified Connecticut steadfastness more than William Williams.

Williams was born in Lebanon, Connecticut, in 1731. His grandfather was the minister of a church for fifty-six years, and his father was pastor of a church at Lebanon for fifty-four years. After graduating from Harvard, Williams studied for the ministry under his father. Although he was very religious and served as a church deacon for forty-three years, William decided not to become a minister. Instead, he became a shopkeeper and entered politics.

At twenty-one, Williams was elected town clerk of Lebanon—a post he held for forty-four years. He also served as a selectman (town official) of Lebanon for twenty-seven years, as a member of the Connecticut legislature's Lower House for about twenty years and the Upper House for twenty-three years, and as a judge for thirty-five years. As was common in his day, Williams held several posts at once. He would have had to live to the age of about 170 to hold all these positions one at a time.

During the revolutionary era, Williams wrote letters to newspapers complaining of British injustice, signing them with such pen names as "America" and "A Friend to His Country." As war came, he wrote that independence was "a Cause unspeakably important," and added that "the Cause of Liberty is the Cause of God."

In late June 1776 Oliver Wolcott had to leave the Continental Congress due to illness. Connecticut sent Williams as Wolcott's substitute. He arrived in Philadelphia on July 28—too late to vote for independence—but on August 2 he signed the Declaration. William Williams served in Congress for about a year.

On Valentine's Day of 1771 William had married Mary Trumbull, daughter of

Connecticut's first state governor, Jonathan Trumbull. William and Mary Williams had three children. During the war the family opened their home to American soldiers and their French allies. Williams purchased supplies for American forces with his own money and reportedly went door to door raising funds and collecting blankets for the army.

A few years after the war, in January 1788, Connecticut held a convention to decide whether or not to approve the U.S. Constitution. Lebanon sent Williams to the convention with instructions that he was to oppose the Constitution. Fortunately, this was one time that William Williams wasn't dependable! Convinced that the new framework of government was best for the country, he ignored his orders and instead voted in favor of the Constitution. Connecticut became our fifth state when Williams and his fellow delegates approved the Constitution on January 9, 1788.

William Williams died at the age of eighty on August 2, 1811—thirty-five years to the day after he had signed the Declaration of Independence.

ROGER SHERMAN:
"Pillar of the Revolution"

Roger Sherman

ONLY ONE MAN SIGNED ALL of these papers that helped establish our nation: the Articles of Association of 1774, the Declaration of Independence, the Articles of Confederation, and the U.S. Constitution. The signer of all four documents was Roger Sherman, whose life was a classic story of a poor boy who made good.

Roger was born in 1721 near Boston, Massachusetts, into a farming family. To earn a living, Roger's father also made shoes. Roger was put to work at his father's cobbler's bench. It was said that as he made shoes Roger kept an open book in front of him so that he could read in his free moments.

When Roger was nineteen, his father died. The Shermans then moved to New Milford, Connecticut, where Roger's oldest brother had settled. According to tradition, Roger walked nearly 150 miles to get there—with his shoemaker's tools on his back!

For a time, Roger continued to farm and make shoes. He also studied to become a surveyor—someone who determines land boundaries. At twenty-four he was appointed surveyor of New Haven County, Connecticut. Roger also ran a country store, became a lawyer, and served as a legislator and a judge. After he was established in Connecticut, he married Elizabeth Hartwell, his sweetheart from his hometown in Massachusetts. The couple had seven children before Elizabeth died at the age of only thirty-four. Roger later married Rebecca Prescott, with whom he had eight more children. Perhaps having fifteen children fostered the traits for which Sherman was known: common sense and fairness.

In 1774 Sherman was sent to the Continental Congress. Some delegates laughed upon meeting him. Instead of a wig, he wore his own brown hair cut short. He had a strong New England accent, and as he spoke he gestured awkwardly with his hands—like a shoemaker pulling a thread, people joked. Yet he won his fellow congressmen's respect with what he said. Sherman was one of the first leaders to assert that Britain had no right to make laws for the thirteen colonies. He was on the committee assigned to create the Declaration, and although his words didn't go into the document, his views did.

Sherman's greatest service to the nation came in 1787, when he helped forge the U.S. Constitution, which replaced the early national laws called the Articles of Confederation. Sherman helped solve a giant problem. The states with large populations wanted to have more lawmakers than those with fewer people. The small states were afraid that if that happened, they wouldn't have much power. Sherman introduced the Connecticut Compromise: Heavily populated states would have more members in the House of Representatives, but each state would have an equal number of U.S. senators. This system was adopted and has worked well for more than two centuries. Sherman's compromise may have inspired Connecticut's nickname, the Constitution State.

Fittingly, Roger Sherman represented Connecticut in the U.S. House of Representatives from 1789 to 1791 and then in the U.S. Senate from 1791 until the time of his death in 1793, at the age of seventy-two. His friend John Adams said that he was "honest as an angel," and called him "one of the soundest and strongest pillars of the Revolution."

VIII. NEW HAMPSHIRE

Englishman Martin Pring, who arrived in 1603, was the first known explorer in New Hampshire. The English named this region of beautiful mountains, woods, and lakes for Hampshire, a county in England. New Hampshire was the third of the thirteen colonies to be permanently settled, after Virginia (1607) and Massachusetts (1620). The British began a settlement at what is now the town of Rye in 1623, and another at Dover around the same time. Strawberry Bank, a settlement founded in 1631, grew into the town of Portsmouth.

New Hampshire is nicknamed the Granite State because of its extensive granite deposits. Hardy people were needed to build farms on its rocky land and survive the cold winters in the northernmost of the thirteen colonies. The colonists cleared the rocks from their fields and used them to build the stone walls that became a New Hampshire trademark. With only about 75,000 settlers by revolutionary times, New Hampshire was one of the least populous colonies.

On January 5, 1776, New Hampshire became the first colony to form its own government completely independent of England. Because the colonies voted from north to south, New Hampshire's congressional delegates were also the first to vote for independence on July 2.

Two New Hampshire signers, Josiah Bartlett and Matthew Thornton, were physicians. The third, William Whipple, became a general in the Revolution. The love of freedom for which New Hampshirites have long been known is expressed in the state motto, Live Free or Die.

NEW HAMPSHIRE

Name	*Birth Date*	*Age at Signing*	*Marriage(s)*	*Children*	*Death Date*	*Age at Death*
Josiah Bartlett	November 21, 1729	46	Mary Bartlett	12	May 19, 1795	65
William Whipple	January 14, 1730	46	Catherine Moffatt	1	November 28, 1785	55
Matthew Thornton	About 1714	About 62	Hannah Jack	5	June 24, 1803	About 89

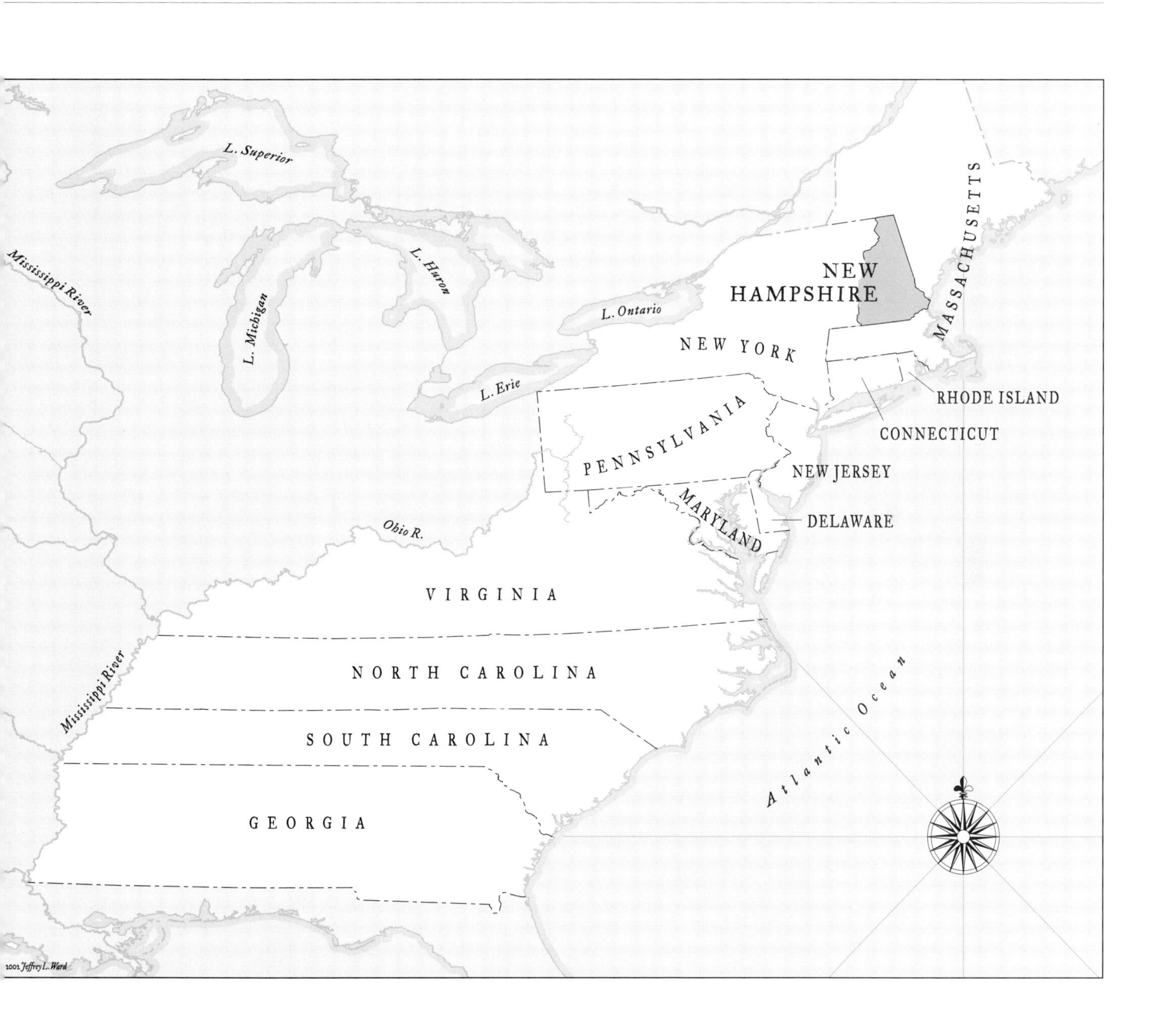

JOSIAH BARTLETT:

The First Vote for Independence

Josiah Bartlett

A NEW HAMPSHIRE MAN HAD the honor of casting the first vote for independence on July 2, 1776.

The youngest of seven children, Josiah Bartlett was born in 1729 in Massachusetts. His parents ran a farm called the Lion's Mouth in Amesbury, located at Massachusetts's northeastern corner. As was the case with Roger Sherman's family, Josiah's father also worked as a shoemaker.

After receiving some schooling from the town teacher, sixteen-year-old Josiah was apprenticed to an Amesbury physician. For about five years, Josiah helped the doctor mix medicines, treat patients, and deliver babies. When Josiah was twenty-one, his master said that he was ready to join the ranks of physicians, and without further ado, he became Dr. Bartlett.

A physician was needed in Kingston, New Hampshire, just ten miles from Amesbury, Bartlett learned. He packed his bags and moved across the border to Kingston, where he set up practice and became known for his ability to treat fevers. In many regions during colonial days almost everyone was related in one way or another, so it wasn't unusual for cousins to marry. In 1754 Josiah married his cousin Mary Bartlett, who then became Mary Bartlett Bartlett. Mary and Josiah had twelve children, eight of whom lived to adulthood.

In 1765 Bartlett was elected to the New Hampshire legislature, where he served until the outbreak of the Revolution and became known as a determined foe of Britain. Dr. Bartlett was chosen to attend the First Continental Congress in 1774 but couldn't go because his house burned down that year and had to be rebuilt. People who resented his support for the patriot cause were believed to have set the fire.

Bartlett was again chosen to represent New Hampshire in the Second Continental Congress in 1775, and this time he went to Philadelphia. As the northernmost colony, New Hampshire often voted first in Congress, and Georgia, as the southernmost, often voted last. On July 2, 1776, Dr. Josiah Bartlett of New Hampshire cast the first vote for independence, and two days later he cast the first vote to approve the Declaration. It is also believed that, after John Hancock, Bartlett was the first delegate to sign the Declaration, which he did in the upper-right-hand corner of the signers' list on August 2. During the war, Bartlett worked in Congress to build the American navy and also treated wounded soldiers.

The U.S. Constitution was created for the new country in 1787. This new framework of government was to take effect when nine states approved it. Josiah Bartlett was instrumental in New Hampshire's approval of the Constitution by a close vote on June 21, 1788. With that vote, New Hampshire became the ninth state, and the U.S. Constitution went into operation. From 1790 to 1794 Bartlett was governor of the Granite State. He died at the age of sixty-five, within a year of leaving his state's highest office. The town of Bartlett, New Hampshire, was named in the signer's honor.

WILLIAM WHIPPLE:
The Signer Who Was a General

A New Hampshire signer fought in the Revolution and rose to the rank of general.

William Whipple was born in what is now Kittery, Maine, in 1730. He went to sea in his teens and by twenty-one was captain of his own ship. Whipple sailed to many ports in Europe, Africa, and the islands off Florida known as the West Indies. At the time, all thirteen colonies allowed slavery. Captain Whipple took part in the slave trade and kept some of the Africans he brought to America as his own house slaves.

At twenty-nine or thirty Whipple gave up the seafaring life. He moved to Portsmouth, New Hampshire, where he worked as a merchant with his brother. In 1767 he married his cousin Catherine Moffatt and went to live in her family home in Portsmouth. The couple's only child died in infancy.

A leading advocate for independence, Whipple helped New Hampshire become the first of the thirteen colonies to form its own government in January 1776. That month he was chosen to represent New Hampshire at the Continental Congress. He took his seat on Leap Year Day—February 29, 1776. A few months later he voted for and signed the Declaration.

Once independence was declared, William Whipple wanted to fight—even though he was starting to suffer from a heart condition that caused him to faint at times. Whipple was one of about sixteen signers who served as soldiers during the war. He rose to the rank of general and took part in campaigns in New York, Massachusetts, and Rhode Island.

It is often forgotten that about 5,000 black men fought on the American side during the Revolution. Many were slaves who had been promised their own liberty as a reward for helping America win its freedom. One of William Whipple's slaves, Prince, fought for America during the war and was freed as promised.

Just two years after the war was won, in 1785, William Whipple died from his heart condition at his home in Portsmouth at the age of fifty-five. Cuffee, his only remaining slave, was freed around the time of Whipple's death.

MATTHEW THORNTON:
"An Honest Man"

Matthew Thornton

DURING A LONG LIFE Matthew Thornton excelled in many fields: as a physician, judge, statesman, writer, and revolutionary patriot.

Thornton was born in Ireland in about 1714. He was one of three signers born on the Emerald Isle, the others being James Smith and George Taylor of Pennsylvania. In 1718, when Matthew was about four, he sailed to America with his family. Their first winter in America the Thorntons had nowhere to live, so they spent those cold months on their ship, anchored along the coast of Maine. Finally they found a home in Worcester, Massachusetts, where Matthew grew up and became a doctor by studying with an established physician.

Young Dr. Thornton moved to Londonderry, New Hampshire, and built up a large medical practice there. He remained a bachelor until age forty-six, when he married Hannah Jack, who was only about eighteen. Matthew and Hannah Thornton would have five children.

Meanwhile, in 1758, Thornton had been sent to New Hampshire's colonial legislature, representing Londonderry. In 1771 he added to his responsibilities by being appointed a judge.

As the arguing with England intensified, the colonies transformed their legislatures into provincial congresses, which were a step toward creating state governments. In early 1775 Matthew Thornton was sent to the New Hampshire Provincial Congress, where he denounced England's policies toward America and won election as the body's president. He worked so intensely on New Hampshire business that at one time he didn't get to change his clothes for ten straight days. Thornton headed the committee that created New Hampshire's first state constitution. Upon its adoption in January 1776, New Hampshire became the first of the original thirteen states to create a government totally independent of the Mother Country.

Matthew Thornton was elected to the Continental Congress in September 1776. Although the independence vote was long past, he signed the Declaration on November 4, 1776—the day he took his seat in Congress. He was one of the last of the fifty-six men to sign the document. The space directly below the signatures of New Hampshire's other two signers was already taken by Samuel Adams of Massachusetts, so Thornton signed his name at the bottom of the right-hand column, apart from Josiah Bartlett and William Whipple.

After serving in the Continental Congress for about a year, Thornton returned to New Hampshire. He no longer practiced medicine, but worked as a judge until his late sixties and served in the state legislature until he was nearly seventy-five. Dr. Thornton then retired to a farm in Merrimack, New Hampshire, where he wrote political articles for newspapers until he was in his eighties.

Matthew Thornton died in 1803 at the age of nearly ninety while visiting his daughter in Massachusetts. On his tombstone was placed the simple tribute, "An Honest Man." The Granite State's little town of Thornton was named for him.

IX. MARYLAND

England settled Virginia, its first American colony, in 1607. The next year Captain John Smith of Virginia went out exploring. On his travels he visited parts of Maryland, including the spot where Baltimore now stands.

In 1631 another Virginian, William Claiborne, began Maryland's first colonial settlement near present-day Annapolis. But Maryland didn't get established as a colony until it was settled by the Calvert family, known as the Lords Baltimore. The Calverts made Maryland a place where Roman Catholics and other persecuted people were welcome. The city of Baltimore, the songbirds called Baltimore orioles, and the Baltimore Orioles baseball team were all named for the Lords Baltimore.

Like Virginia, Maryland produced huge amounts of tobacco. Most Marylanders lived in small houses and wore homespun clothes, but the well-to-do built large estates called manors, where slaves grew the crops. By the mid-1770s, Maryland was home to 220,000 people, about a third of them slaves.

Four Marylanders signed the Declaration: Samuel Chase, William Paca, Thomas Stone, and Charles Carroll of Carrollton. Maryland was nicknamed the Old Line State because George Washington praised the bravery of its "troops of the line," or soldiers. Washington, D.C., which became the country's permanent capital in 1800, was carved out of a chunk of the Old Line State.

MARYLAND

Name	*Birth Date*	*Age at Signing*	*Marriage(s)*	*Children*	*Death Date*	*Age at Death*
Samuel Chase	April 17, 1741	35	Anne Baldwin Hannah Kitty Giles	9	June 19, 1811	70
William Paca	October 31, 1740	35	Mary Chew Anne Harrison	4	October 13, 1799	58
Thomas Stone	1743	About 33	Margaret Brown	At least 3	October 5, 1787	About 44
Charles Carroll of Carrollton	September 19, 1737	38	Mary Darnall	7	November 14, 1832	95

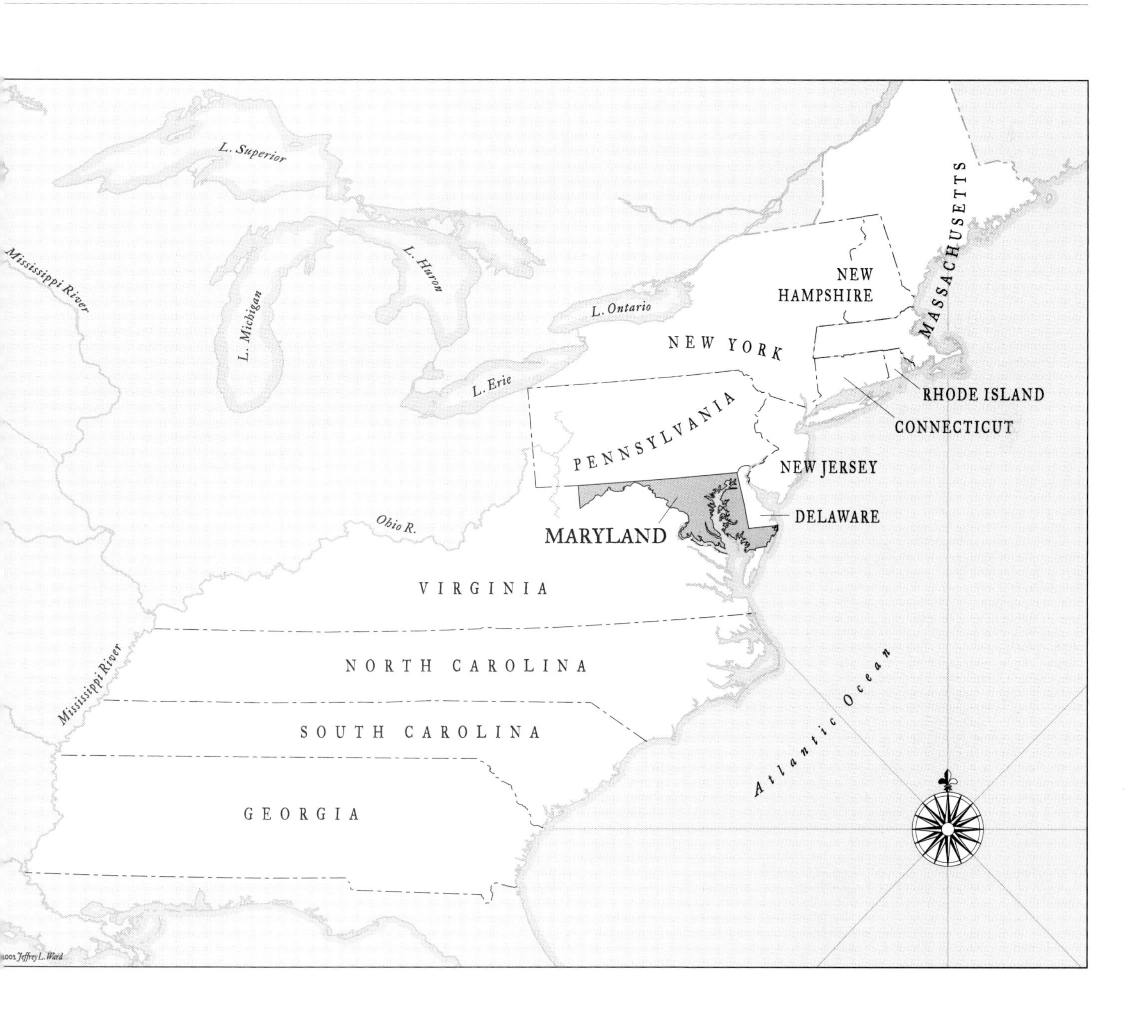

SAMUEL CHASE:
"The Torch That Lit the Revolutionary Flame"

Samuel Chase

No signer stirred up more controversy or had a more fiery temperament than a Marylander known as "Bacon Face."

Samuel Chase was born in Maryland's Somerset County in 1741. His mother died soon after his birth, and at the age of three "Sammy" moved to Baltimore with his father, who was a minister. Sammy received his early schooling from his father before studying law in Annapolis. At twenty he became an attorney, and the next year he married Anne Baldwin, with whom he had seven children.

Chase won a seat in the Maryland legislature at the age of only twenty-three. He was a man who did what he thought was right—regardless of the consequences. For example, he voted for a measure regulating ministers' pay—even though it cut his father's salary in half!

An ardent patriot, Chase organized the Sons of Liberty in the Annapolis region with his friend William Paca. In late 1765 Annapolis patriots created a dummy that resembled a British tax officer. To show what they thought of the British stamp tax, the patriots decided to burn the dummy. The honor of putting the torch to it went to Samuel Chase. People who sided with England were "despicable," Chase said, adding that they belonged in a "dunghill." They retaliated by calling him a "ringleader of mobs" and a "foul-mouthed son of discord." Because of his ruddy complexion, which grew even redder when he was excited, Chase was given another nickname: "Bacon Face."

In 1774 Maryland sent Chase to the Continental Congress. Two years later he, Benjamin Franklin, Charles Carroll of Carrollton, and John Carroll visited Canada but could not convince the Canadians to fight on America's side.

Chase returned to Philadelphia to find Congress discussing independence. The problem was, the patriot leaders back in Maryland hadn't granted permission for their delegates in Congress to vote for separation from England. Chase rushed home and convinced them to change their minds. He then rode more than a hundred miles back to Philadelphia in two days, arriving just in time to vote for independence. For his zeal in the cause he was called the "Samuel Adams of Maryland" and "the torch that lit the Revolutionary flame in Maryland."

After the war, Chase became a judge back in Maryland. His wife Anne had died during the war. In 1784 he married Hannah Kitty Giles, with whom he had two more children.

In 1796 President George Washington appointed Chase to the U.S. Supreme Court, where he served the last fifteen years of his life. Today he is remembered as one of the finest justices in the early years of our nation's highest court. But in his own time he made many enemies because of his hot temper and his political views. For example, he angered supporters of President Jefferson by speaking out against his policies. The House of Representatives impeached him (charged him with misconduct) in 1804. The next year, in a heated Senate trial, Chase was found not guilty, allowing hm to retain his position on the high court. This helped establish the precedent that judges shouldn't be removed for political reasons. The Maryland firebrand died in Baltimore in 1811 at the age of seventy.

WILLIAM PACA:
"Millions Yet Unborn"

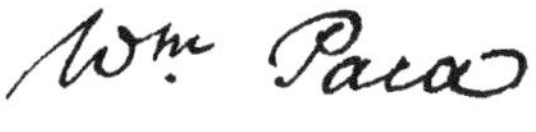

Wm. Paca

LONG BEFORE ANY OF US WERE ALIVE, William Paca thought of us. Once when writing to George Washington, he borrowed Samuel Adams's expression and declared that they were fighting for "millions yet unborn."

Paca (pronounced *PAKE-uh*) was born into a wealthy family on Halloween of 1740, not far from Baltimore. At twelve, he entered the school that became the University of Pennsylvania. Following graduation, he studied law in Annapolis, then completed his legal training in England. William settled in Annapolis, married Mary Chew, and became one of Maryland's leading attorneys. In court he was often opposed by his close friend Samuel Chase.

Paca and Chase both sided with America against the Mother Country, but their styles were different. While Chase stirred up crowds with his fiery speeches, Paca, a quiet man, preferred to write newspaper articles and work behind the scenes. Together, they were a great team that helped lead Maryland toward independence.

In 1767 Paca was elected to represent Annapolis in the Maryland legislature. Later he represented Maryland in the Continental Congress, where he signed the Declaration. Paca meant it when he pledged his life, fortune, and sacred honor. He spent thousands of dollars of his own funds to supply the American troops during the war. From 1782 to 1785 he served as Maryland's governor.

When the U.S. Constitution was created in 1787, many Americans complained that it didn't protect certain basic rights. The Bill of Rights that was added to the Constitution to remedy this contained several of William Paca's suggestions. These included provisions for freedom of religion, freedom of the press, and legal protection for citizens accused of crimes.

William Paca suffered much personal tragedy. His wife Mary died at the age of thirty-eight, and only one of their three children lived to adulthood. William remarried, but his second wife, Anne Harrison Paca, died at twenty-three, and their only child didn't reach his third birthday. Paca had two other children with women he didn't marry. One of them, his daughter Hester, was born to a black woman. Paca helped raise Hester and sent her to one of the finest boarding schools in Philadelphia.

In later life Paca was one of America's wealthiest men. By 1790 he owned more than 100 slaves. Around then he built Wye Hall, which was said to be the nation's most magnificent mansion. Lonely in his last years, William Paca died on his huge estate about three weeks before what would have been his fifty-ninth birthday.

THOMAS STONE:
A Quiet Man Who Hated War

Thos. Stone

THOMAS STONE WAS ANOTHER OF THE HANDFUL of signers about whom very little is known.

Stone was born in Charles County, Maryland, not far from present-day Washington, D.C., in 1743. He borrowed money to study law in the office of Thomas Johnson, who later became Maryland's first state governor. For several years Stone practiced law in Frederick, Maryland. At twenty-five he married Margaret Brown, with whom he had at least three children. Seeking a quiet life, the Stones settled on a farm in Thomas's native Charles County in 1771.

The times would not permit the peaceful life Thomas Stone craved. By the early 1770s, he had made a name for himself as an opponent of British policies toward the colonies. In December 1774 he was elected to the Continental Congress. He reluctantly left home, journeyed to Philadelphia, and took his seat the following May.

Stone rarely spoke in Congress, and, while he sided with his country, he dreaded the prospect of a long, bloody war with the Mother Country. Even a few months after he had voted for and signed the Declaration, Stone still favored finding some way to make peace with Britain.

While in Congress, Thomas Stone served on the committee that created the Articles of Confederation, the governmental framework that bound the new country together during the Revolution. The articles remained in effect from 1781 until the late 1780s, when the new U.S. Constitution replaced them.

During his last few years, Thomas Stone served in the Maryland State Senate. He was also elected to represent Maryland at the convention held in Philadelphia in 1787 to create the U.S. Constitution. But this time he didn't go to Philadelphia because he would not leave his wife, who was extremely ill. Margaret Stone died in June 1787. Thomas was so grief-stricken that he gave up his law practice.

Just four months after his wife's passing, Thomas Stone died at the age of about forty-four. People claimed that the quiet man who hated war and loved his family had died of grief.

CHARLES CARROLL OF CARROLLTON:

"The Last of the Signers"

Charles Carroll of Carrollton

THE FIFTY-SIX SIGNERS INCLUDED THE MAN who was reputedly America's richest person.

Charles Carroll, the only child of a wealthy tobacco planter, was born in Annapolis in 1737. He often suffered from fevers and chills and didn't seem destined to live long—or so people believed.

The Carrolls, who were of Irish Catholic heritage, were treated as second-class citizens despite their wealth. By the 1700s the spirit of religious tolerance had been discarded in Maryland, and the colony had laws barring Catholics from voting, operating their own schools, or practicing law. Nevertheless, a few priests secretly ran Catholic schools in private homes in Maryland. Charles Carroll attended one of these secret schools and at age ten was sent to Europe to continue his education.

Charles spent the next eighteen years abroad. He returned to Maryland in 1765, just as the troubles with England began. Three years later, in 1768, he married his cousin Mary Darnall, with whom he had seven children.

Many people expected wealthy young Charles Carroll to side with England, where he had spent part of his time overseas. But he resented the Mother Country for oppressing Catholics in both Ireland and the American colonies. Carroll decided to risk his life and his fortune seeking independence, which he called "the best and most glorious cause" in a letter to George Washington.

Carroll began writing anti-British articles for the *Maryland Gazette* in 1773. In October 1774 the *Peggy Stewart* came to Annapolis carrying British tea. "Set fire to the vessel!" Carroll reportedly told Maryland patriots, who then forced the *Peggy Stewart*'s owner to burn his own ship.

In the spring of 1776 the Continental Congress sent Carroll, fellow Marylanders Samuel Chase and John Carroll (Charles's cousin), and Benjamin Franklin to Canada in an unsuccessful attempt to persuade the Canadians to help America win the war. On July 4, 1776, a few days after his return, Carroll was elected to Congress. It was too late to vote, but in August he placed his usual signature—"Charles Carroll of Carrollton"—on the Declaration. Carrollton was one of his estates. The wealthy Maryland patriot signed this way to distinguish himself from relatives who were also named Charles Carroll. He was the only Catholic signer.

Also in 1776, Charles Carroll helped frame Maryland's first state constitution. Later he served as one of the Old Line State's first two U.S. senators. And although the man who was said to be America's wealthiest person owned hundreds of slaves, Carroll eventually turned against slavery. Now and then he freed some slaves, including thirty at a time when he was eighty.

Charles Carroll, who had been frail and sickly in his youth, rode his horse ten miles a day at age ninety-three. During his last few years, he was the only living signer of the Declaration of Independence. Strangers came by just to shake his hand or catch a glimpse of him. In 1832 "the Last of the signers" died at his daughter's home in Baltimore, at the age of ninety-five.

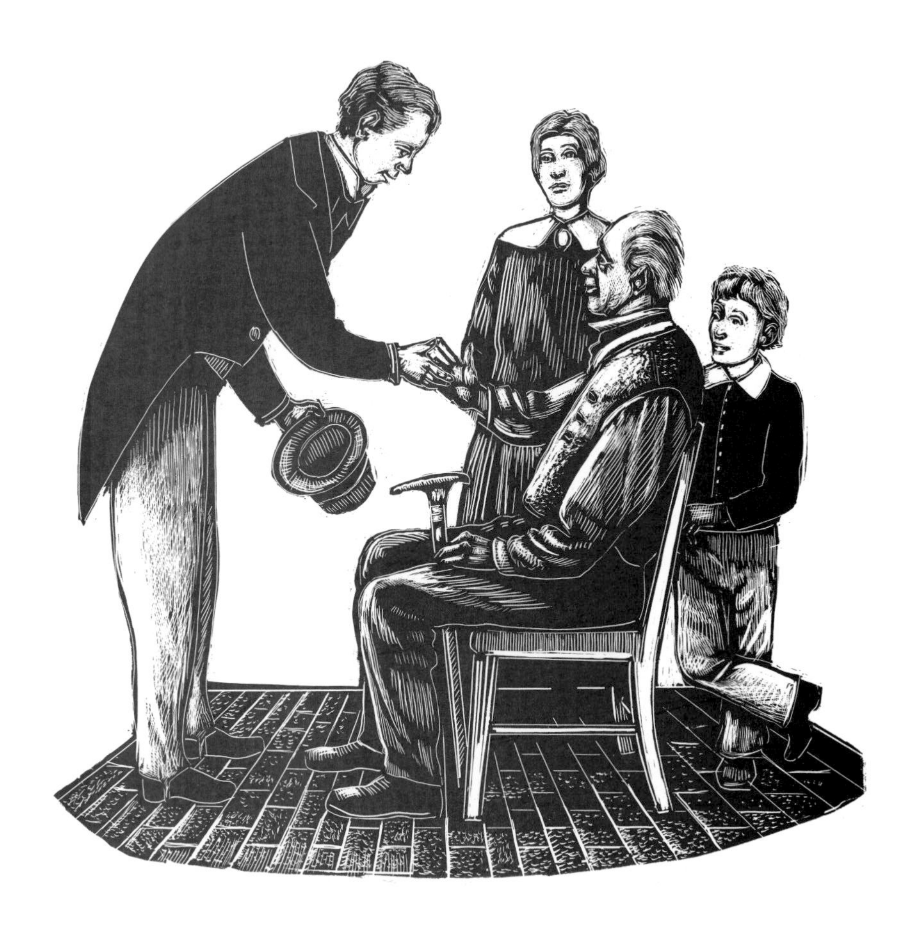

X. NORTH CAROLINA

Long before Jamestown, Virginia, was founded in 1607 as its first *permanent* American settlement, England tried without success to settle what is now North Carolina. Colonists arrived there in 1585 and began England's first North American settlement, but a food shortage and other hardships led to its abandonment. Another group of settlers arrived at North Carolina's Roanoke Island in July 1587. The next month colonist Eleanor Dare gave birth to a daughter named Virginia Dare, who was the first English child born in America. The colony soon disappeared, however. Its members may have gone to live with, or been killed by, Indians. Because their fate remains a mystery, Virginia Dare and her fellow settlers are known as the Lost Colony.

North Carolina's first permanent settlers came from Virginia in the 1650s. Many of the early colonists were poor farmers who grew corn and a little tobacco. By the mid-1770s, North Carolina ranked fourth in population with 230,000 colonists, including 80,000 slaves.

In October 1774 women in Edenton, North Carolina, pledged that they would not drink British tea or wear British clothes. A few months later, in March 1775, women in Wilmington, North Carolina, burned British tea. These were among the first important political acts by American women of the Revolutionary era. Then, on April 12, 1776, North Carolina's revolutionary government became the first to tell its congressional delegates to vote for independence. William Hooper, John Penn, and Joseph Hewes signed the Declaration for the Tar Heel State, as North Carolina was nicknamed for reasons that have long been debated.

NORTH CAROLINA

Name	Birth Date	Age at Signing	Marriage(s)	Children	Death Date	Age at Death
William Hooper	June 17, 1742	34	Anne Clark	3	October 14, 1790	48
ohn Penn	May 6, 1740	36	Susannah Lyme	2 or 3	September 14, 1788	48
oseph Hewes	January 23, 1730	46	Never married	0	November 10, 1779	49

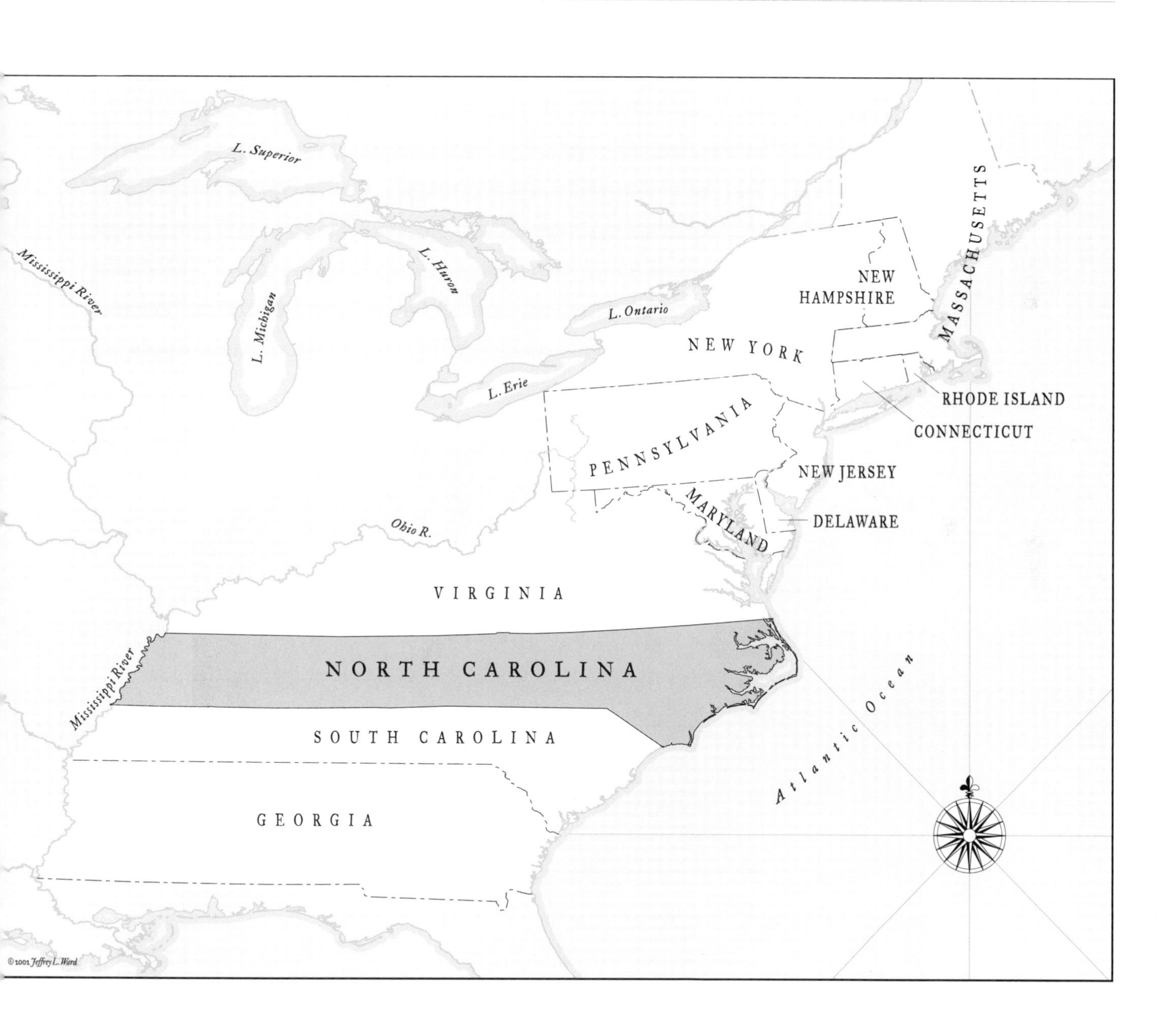

WILLIAM HOOPER:
"Striding Fast to Independence"

Wm Hooper

THE REVOLUTION DIVIDED many colonial families, some members siding with America and others with Britain. William Hooper of North Carolina experienced this situation—twice.

William was born in Boston, Massachusetts, in 1742. His father wanted him to become a minister like himself, but William had other plans. He graduated from Harvard at eighteen, then studied law under James Otis, a leading Boston attorney who popularized the slogan, "Taxation without representation is tyranny!" It is believed that some of Otis's rebelliousness rubbed off on his student.

Hooper completed his law studies and in 1764 moved to Wilmington, North Carolina, to practice. One reason he settled 700 miles to the south was that Boston had too many lawyers. Perhaps he also wanted to avoid conflicts with relatives who remained loyal to Britain. Soon Hooper became one of North Carolina's leading attorneys. At twenty-five he married Anne Clark of Wilmington, with whom he had a daughter and two sons. In one way his life didn't change, however. Some of Anne's relatives were Loyalists, and a number of the couple's friends also maintained their loyalty to the Mother Country.

In 1773 Hooper was elected to North Carolina's colonial legislature, where he became a spokesman for America's rights. The thirteen colonies were "striding fast to independence, and ere long will build an empire upon the ruins of Great Britain," he wrote to a friend in 1774. That year North Carolina sent him to the Continental Congress, where he served until 1777. Hooper was away from Philadelphia during the vote on independence, but returned in time for the big signing on August 2.

William Hooper received abuse from all sides during the revolutionary era. The British burned his home, and he had to flee to the North Carolina backcountry to avoid being captured by the enemy. Loyalist friends and relatives were furious with him for taking the patriot side. And because he favored dealing gently with the Loyalists instead of punishing them, some patriots falsely accused him of being a Loyalist himself. Moreover, the hardships of war contributed to a decline in his health, and he became seriously ill with malaria.

Hooper served in the Tar Heel State's legislature during and after the war. Having long suffered from poor health that was made worse by heavy drinking, William Hooper died in 1790 at the age of just forty-eight.

JOHN PENN:
"My First Wish Is That America May Be Free"

John Penn

WHILE BATTLING BRITAIN, the patriots often argued among themselves over politics, military strategy, and personal matters. A North Carolina signer was challenged to a duel by a president of the Continental Congress.

John Penn was born in Virginia in 1740. Despite having the same last name, he and William Penn, the founder of Pennsylvania, were probably not related. However, John was a cousin of Edmund Pendleton, a lawyer who became a leading Virginia patriot. John studied law under his cousin, then went to work as an attorney in Virginia. At twenty-three, Penn married Susannah Lyme, with whom he had at least two and perhaps three children.

Like Massachusetts, Virginia had plenty of lawyers. Looking for a place where he would have more clients, Penn moved with his family across the border to Granville County, North Carolina, in 1774. There he became a leader of the local patriots. In 1775 Penn was elected to represent North Carolina in the Continental Congress, where he served for five years. For a while he hoped that Britain and America would make up, but once he realized that wouldn't happen, he came out for independence. In early 1776 he wrote from Philadelphia, "My first wish is that America may be free."

As July 2, 1776, approached, some of the home governments told their delegates in Congress how to vote. That April, the North Carolina Provincial Congress became the first home government to instruct its delegates to vote for separation from Britain. John Penn gladly did so, and a month after casting his vote signed the Declaration along with his two fellow North Carolinians.

John Penn had an argument over political issues with Henry Laurens of South Carolina, who was president of the Continental Congress from late 1777 to late 1778. In those days, men who quarreled sometimes fought duels, which could end in death. Vice President Aaron Burr killed Alexander Hamilton in a famous pistol duel in 1804, and signer Button Gwinnett also fought a deadly duel. Laurens challenged John Penn to a pistol duel.

According to one story, once the heat of anger had passed, neither man wanted to fight, but they couldn't find a way to back down gracefully. Since Laurens and Penn lived at the same boardinghouse, they ate breakfast together on the morning they were scheduled to duel. While headed to an empty lot in Philadelphia to fight, they came to a muddy place. Penn helped Laurens, who was much older than himself, across the ditch. Suddenly Penn realized that they were being foolish, and patched up his quarrel with Henry Laurens on the spot. According to another version of the story, they actually fired their guns at each other on the dueling field, but fortunately, neither man was shot. They then separated, each satisfied that he had upheld his personal honor.

Penn left Congress in 1780, then returned home and served as the leading member of North Carolina's Board of War at the end of the Revolution. This was a tragic period in North Carolina, as the state's Loyalists and patriots burned each other's farms and killed one another. By the time peace came, Penn was in failing health. John Penn died at the age of forty-eight in 1788.

JOSEPH HEWES:
"To Die or Be Free"

Joseph Hewes,

A North Carolina signer was one of the main founders of what is now the U.S. Navy.

Like North Carolina's other two signers, Joseph Hewes came from outside the colony. He was born into a Quaker family in New Jersey in 1730. For a number of years he worked as an apprentice to a Philadelphia merchant. At twenty-five he moved to Edenton, North Carolina, where he became a successful merchant who sent ships to many ports. A friend referred to Hewes as one of "the best and most agreeable men in the world," but something happened to change his cheerful outlook. Just days before he was to marry a young woman named Isabella Johnston, she died. Brokenhearted, Joseph Hewes never married.

For about ten years before the Revolution, Hewes served in North Carolina's colonial legislature. In 1774 he was elected to the Continental Congress, where he held a seat on and off until almost the last day of his life, often laboring from dawn to dusk without pausing to eat or drink. Because of his experience with shipping, he ran the committee that helped establish the navy. This made him in effect the first secretary of the navy, although that title didn't yet exist. Back in North Carolina, Hewes had developed great admiration for a sea captain named John Paul Jones. Thanks to Hewes, Jones was appointed as an officer in the Continental Navy in December 1775. John Paul Jones would become America's greatest naval hero of the war.

His war efforts brought Hewes more heartache. The Quakers, who hated war, denounced the Continental Congress in 1775. Joseph Hewes broke with the Quaker faith and never returned.

Inwardly, Hewes was torn by the prospect of independence. "Every American is determined to die or be free," he wrote to a friend, but added that a permanent break with England might be too bold a step. Even after several battles had been fought and Hewes had helped establish the navy, he hesitated about independence. His vote on July 2 would be vitally important. William Hooper was away, so if John Penn voted for independence and Joseph Hewes voted against it, North Carolina would be locked in a one-one tie.

According to John Adams, in the midst of the debates on independence, Hewes suddenly rose from his chair and declared that he would vote for separation from England. Lifting his hands as if in prayer, Hewes cried out, "It is done, and I will abide by it!" Joseph Hewes and John Penn both voted for independence on July 2, and a month later they and William Hooper signed the Declaration.

Joseph Hewes lived for just a little more than three years after signing. Illness forced him to leave Congress on October 29, 1779, and twelve days later he died at the age of forty-nine. It was believed that his death was caused by overwork, and that he had given his life to help make his country free.

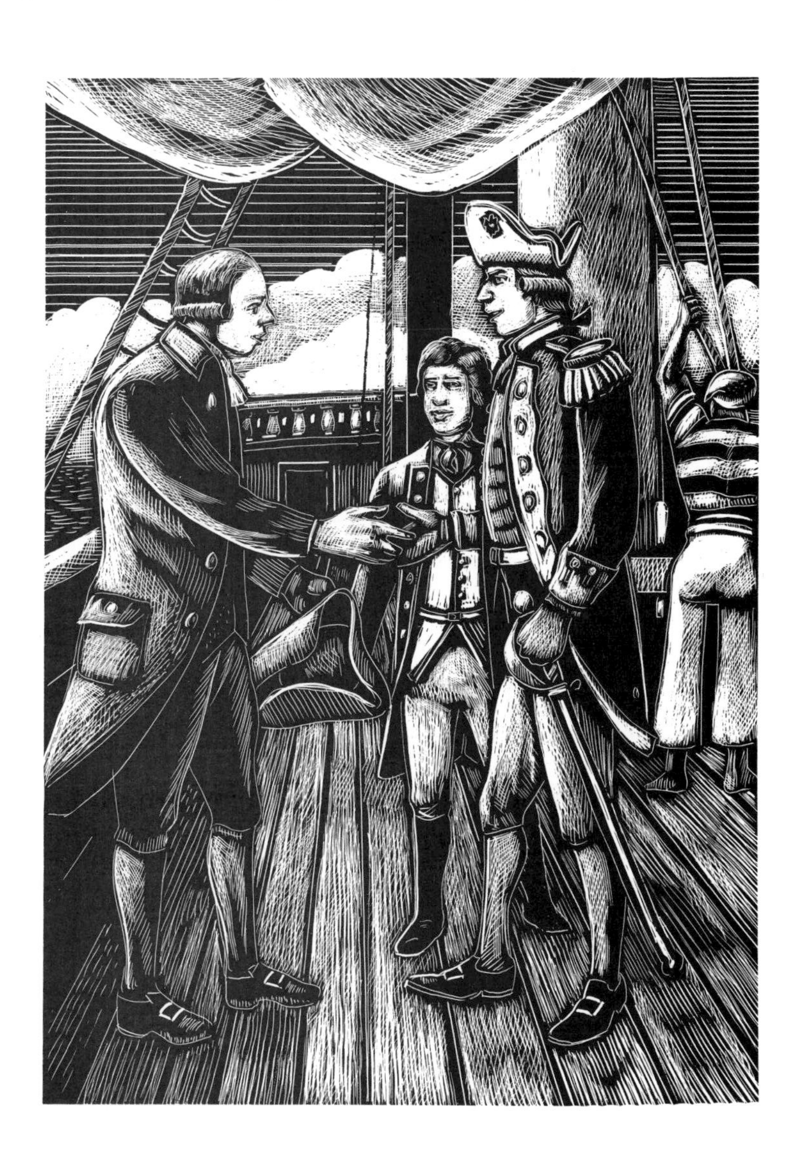

XI. SOUTH CAROLINA

Spanish explorers arrived in what is now South Carolina in 1521. Five years later, Spaniards began the first European colony in what is now the United States along South Carolina's coast, probably near present-day Georgetown. Like North Carolina's "Lost Colony," it did not last. Disease and hunger quickly brought it to an end.

South Carolina's first permanent colonists were English. In 1670 settlers from England arrived and began South Carolina's first colonial town that lasted—Charleston. The colonists discovered that rice grew well in South Carolina's swampy coastlands. A South Carolina teenager named Eliza Lucas Pinckney experimented with growing indigo, a plant that was used to make a blue dye. Eliza grew a good indigo crop in 1744, and soon other planters were growing it too. Rice and indigo helped make South Carolina a wealthy colony, with lovely plantations here and there. By the mid-1770s the colony was home to about 150,000 settlers, slightly more than half of them slaves. Charleston, with 12,000 people, was the fourth-largest city in the thirteen colonies.

Edward Rutledge, Thomas Lynch Jr., Thomas Heyward Jr., and Arthur Middleton signed the Declaration of Independence for South Carolina. A Revolutionary War battle inspired the state's nickname. In 1776 English ships attacked a fort guarding Charleston. The enemy thought the fort would soon fall, but their cannonballs just sank into its soft walls, which had been made of logs from palmetto trees. The Americans won this battle, and South Carolina became known as the Palmetto State.

SOUTH CAROLINA

Name	*Birth Date*	*Age at Signing*	*Marriage(s)*	*Children*	*Death Date*	*Age at Death*
EDWARD RUTLEDGE	November 23, 1749	26	Henrietta Middleton Mary Shubrick Everleigh	3	January 23, 1800	50
THOMAS LYNCH JR.	August 5, 1749	Near his 27th birthday	Elizabeth Shubrick	0	Late 1779	30
THOMAS HEYWARD JR.	July 28, 1746	30	Elizabeth Mathewes Elizabeth Savage	8	March or April, 1809	62
ARTHUR MIDDLETON	June 26, 1742	34	Mary Izard	9	January 1, 1787	44

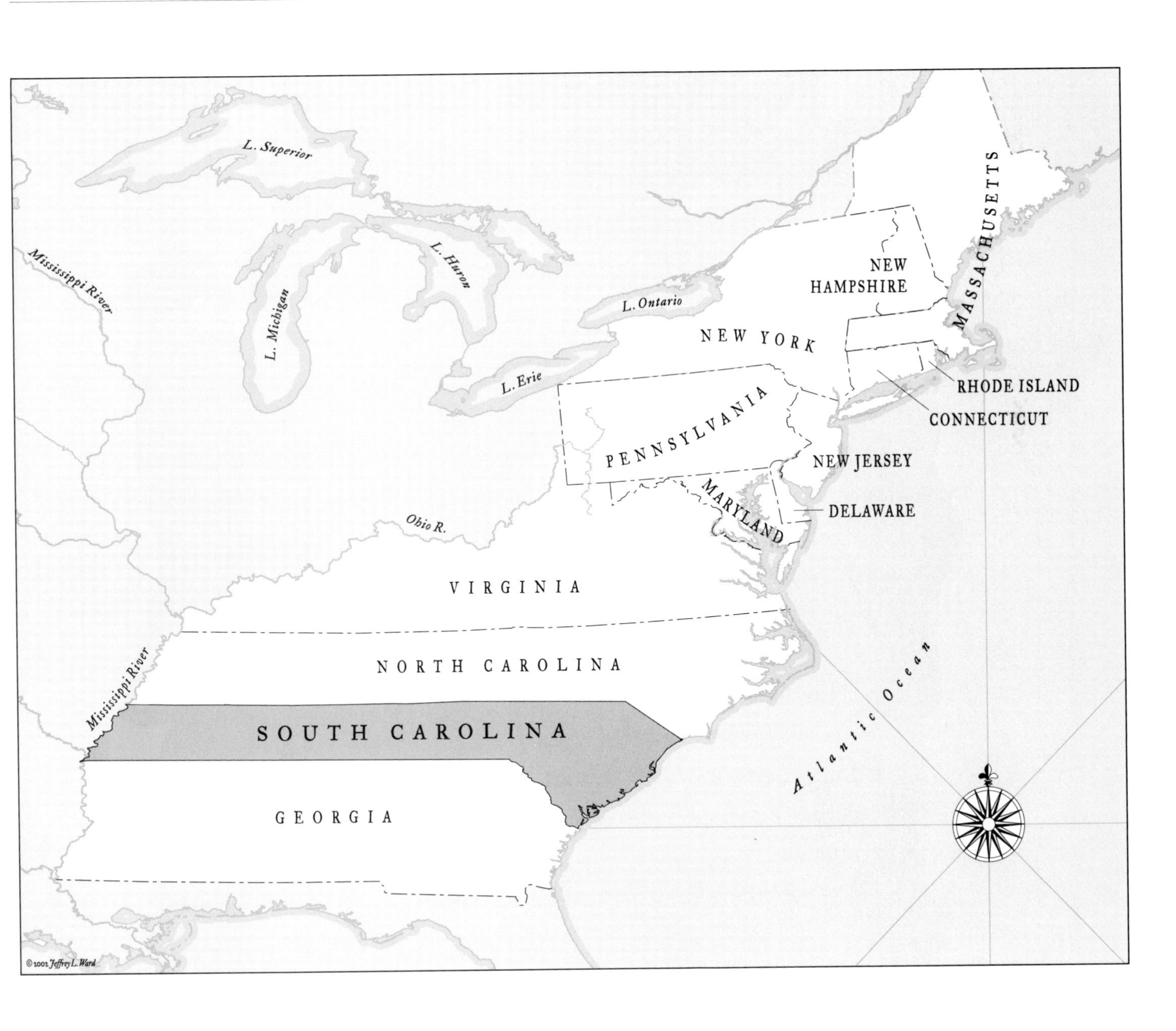

EDWARD RUTLEDGE:
The Youngest Signer

Edward Rutledge Jr.

THE MEN WHO HELPED ESTABLISH the United States are sometimes called the Founding Fathers. This nickname makes them sound rather old, but actually several of them were quite young. The two youngest signers both came from South Carolina.

Edward Rutledge was born near Charleston, South Carolina, on November 23, 1749. Ned, as he was called, studied law with his older brother John, then continued his legal studies in England. He returned home in 1773 and the next year married Henrietta Middleton, a member of a prominent South Carolina family. The couple had three children.

Ned Rutledge made a name as a patriot by his legal work on behalf of a printer who had defied British laws. In 1774 he was elected as a delegate to the Continental Congress. "Young Ned Rutledge," John Adams said of the wealthy South Carolinian, was "a peacock." He was referring to the fact that Ned dressed in fancy clothes and had a proud manner, which could also be said of South Carolina's other three signers.

On July 1, 1776, when the trial vote was taken, South Carolina rejected independence. Edward Rutledge helped convince the colony's delegation to change its vote the next day. At twenty-six years old, he was the youngest signer. Ned's brother-in-law Arthur Middleton also signed the Declaration, which meant that Henrietta Middleton Rutledge had a husband and a brother who were both signers. Meanwhile, Ned's brother John Rutledge, who had taught him law, was serving as South Carolina's first state governor.

Ned Rutledge returned home in late 1776 to help defend his state. When the British seized Charleston in the spring of 1780, Rutledge was among those captured. He spent about a year in Florida as a prisoner. To further punish the Rutledges for their role in the Revolution, their mother, Sarah Hext Rutledge, was taken from her home and imprisoned in Charleston.

After the war, Rutledge served in the South Carolina state legislature for many years. His wife Henrietta died in 1792, and later that year he married Mary Shubrick Everleigh. From 1798 to 1800 Rutledge was governor of the Palmetto State, as his brother John had been about twenty years earlier.

George Washington died on December 14, 1799. Governor Edward Rutledge suffered a stroke soon after—reportedly because he was so upset by Washington's death. The man who had been the youngest signer died in January 1800 at the age of fifty.

THOMAS LYNCH JR.:
His Father Almost Signed, Too

Thomas Lynch Junr

IF NOT FOR THE ILLNESS OF THE OLDER MAN, a father and son would have both signed the Declaration of Independence.

While representing South Carolina in the Continental Congress, Thomas Lynch Sr. suffered a stroke on February 20, 1776. He had one son, Thomas Lynch Jr. Born near Georgetown, South Carolina, on August 5, 1749, the younger Lynch had studied law in England, returned home and married Elizabeth Shubrick, and settled down to a life as a wealthy planter and lawmaker. At the start of the war Thomas Jr. served in the army. While in North Carolina he became ill with what may have been malaria, which severely weakened him and turned him into a partial invalid for the rest of his life.

In March 1776 the South Carolina legislature selected Thomas Lynch Jr. to go to Congress as an additional delegate for the colony. This was done partly so that he might care for his father, and partly because he had proven himself to be a patriot and soldier in his own right. Despite suffering from poor health himself, Thomas Jr. managed to make the 600-mile trip to Philadelphia.

Upon his arrival, he found that his father was too ill to continue in Congress. Thomas Jr. remained in Philadelphia and served in Congress long enough to vote for independence and sign the Declaration around the time of his twenty-seventh birthday. He was the second-youngest signer, after Edward Rutledge. On the Declaration, a space was saved between the signatures of Edward Rutledge and Thomas Heyward Jr., where Thomas Lynch Sr. would have signed had he been able. Thomas Sr. reportedly improved somewhat under his son's care, but not enough to appear in Congress to sign the Declaration.

In late 1776 the father and son headed home. Thomas Sr. wasn't able to complete the journey. While stopping in Annapolis, Maryland, with his son in December, Thomas Sr. suffered another stroke that proved fatal.

Thomas Lynch Jr. reached home, but his own health was failing rapidly. Hoping that a change in climate would help him recover, Thomas and his wife Elizabeth embarked on an ocean voyage in late 1779. Their ship was lost at sea. The second-youngest signer was just thirty years old when he and his wife perished. The couple left no children.

THOMAS HEYWARD JR.:
"God Save the States"

Thos Heyward Junr.

THOMAS HEYWARD JR. WAS WOUNDED and imprisoned fighting for independence. Ironically, as late as July 1, 1776, he wasn't even sure that he favored separation from England.

Heyward was born near Beaufort, South Carolina, in 1746. His father's name was Daniel, not Thomas, but since the family had other Thomas Heywards, the future signer added a Jr. to the end of his name to distinguish himself.

A member of one of South Carolina's wealthiest families, Thomas had every advantage. He studied law in the Mother Country, where he was annoyed to find that the English looked down on Americans. After returning home he became a successful lawyer, built a plantation called White Hall, and in 1772 was elected to the South Carolina legislature. The next year he married Elizabeth Mathewes, sister of South Carolina governor John Mathews. (The sister and brother spelled their last name differently.) Thomas and Elizabeth had five children.

Heyward was elected to represent South Carolina in the Continental Congress in February 1776. Although he was angry at England for many reasons, Heyward and the other South Carolina delegates weren't certain that America was ready to stand alone. South Carolina's delegates rejected independence in the July 1 trial vote, but switched their votes the next day so as not to divide the country. A month later Heyward and his fellow South Carolinians signed the Declaration. Thomas Heyward Jr. was just a few days past his thirtieth birthday when he placed his John Hancock on the document.

Later in the war, Heyward returned to South Carolina to fight the British. In early 1779 he was wounded while helping to win a battle on Port Royal Island, near Beaufort, South Carolina. He recovered, and a year later he helped defend

Charleston. When the British seized the city in May 1780, he was among those captured. For about a year he was imprisoned in Saint Augustine, Florida. It was said that, while imprisoned, he made up a song called "God Save the States" and taught it to the other American prisoners. During the war, the enemy plundered his estate, White Hall. They seized and carried away all of his slaves, 130 of whom were reportedly sold to the sugar plantations of Jamaica.

After he was freed, Heyward served as a judge and state lawmaker in South Carolina. His wife died in 1782, and four years later he remarried. With his second wife, Elizabeth Savage Heyward, he had three more children.

The South Carolina signer who had hesitated about independence and then done so much to win it died in 1809 at the age of sixty-two.

ARTHUR MIDDLETON:

"All His Zeal in This Cause"

Arthur Middleton

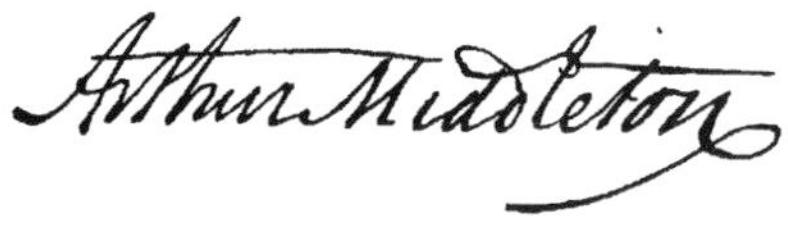

THREE OF THE SOUTH CAROLINIANS—Edward Rutledge, Thomas Lynch Jr., and Thomas Heyward Jr.—were thirty or younger when they signed the Declaration. Arthur Middleton, the oldest of South Carolina's four signers, was just thirty-four—less than half the age of Benjamin Franklin.

Arthur was born at Middleton Place, a plantation near Charleston, in 1742. His family was immensely rich. Henry Middleton, his father, owned more than twenty plantations covering 50,000 acres (about eighty square miles), and approximately 800 slaves.

At the age of twelve, Arthur was sent to England, where he attended school and studied law. He returned home just before Christmas of 1763 after nine years abroad and the next year married Mary Izard, with whom he would have nine children. In 1765 Arthur Middleton was elected to the South Carolina legislature.

While Arthur was helping to organize resistance to Britain in South Carolina, his father was sent to the Continental Congress in 1774, and briefly served as its president that fall. Citing his health as the reason, Henry Middleton turned down a reappointment to Congress in early 1776. Arthur, who was considered more of a revolutionary, was elected to replace him.

Arthur took his seat in Philadelphia by May 20. John Adams wrote that Arthur Middleton had "all his zeal in this cause," referring to America's struggle with England. He was part of the South Carolina delegation that switched its vote to independence on July 2. The next month, Arthur Middleton signed the Declaration—with one of the prettiest signatures on the document.

Like Edward Rutledge and Thomas Heyward Jr., Arthur Middleton defended Charleston against enemy attack in 1780. And like them, he was seized when the city fell and was held captive in Florida for many months. Meanwhile, the enemy plundered his property and carried off 200 of his slaves, who were later sold in the islands of the West Indies. It was said that Mary Izard Middleton had to beg help from the British to care for her children during her husband's imprisonment.

Following the war, Arthur Middleton repaired the damage done to his property. He only briefly enjoyed the victory he had helped achieve. On New Year's Day of 1787 Arthur Middleton died, at the age of only forty-four.

XII. GEORGIA

Explorer Hernando de Soto of Spain arrived in what is now Georgia in 1540 while searching for gold. The Spanish built a fort in present-day Georgia in 1566, but did little to settle the region.

By the early 1700s England ruled twelve American colonies, from Maine (then part of Massachusetts) to South Carolina. Englishman James Oglethorpe wanted to build a new American colony, and received permission from King George II to start a thirteenth colony south of South Carolina. Oglethorpe and about 120 settlers left England on the *Anne* in November 1732. Early the next year they founded Savannah, Georgia's first permanent colonial town. Augusta and other towns were soon started in the new colony, which was named Georgia for Britain's King George II.

Oglethorpe hated slavery, which his colony outlawed at first. But in 1743 he returned to England, and seven years later Georgia's ban on slavery was lifted. Farms were built where Georgians grew rice and other crops with slave labor. By 1775 Georgia had about 40,000 colonists, more than a third of whom were slaves. Georgia and Delaware were tied as the colonies with the smallest populations.

During the revolutionary era, Georgia had the highest percentage of Loyalists of the thirteen colonies. This was because the youngest colony was home to many people who had been born in the Mother Country and still thought of themselves as English. However, many Georgians, especially younger people, fought bravely for independence. All three Georgia signers—Lyman Hall, Button Gwinnett, and George Walton—later served as governor of what became known as the Peach State.

GEORGIA

Name	*Birth Date*	*Age at Signing*	*Marriage(s)*	*Children*	*Death Date*	*Age at Death*
Lyman Hall	April 12, 1724	52	Abigail Burr Mary Osborne	1	October 19, 1790	66
Button Gwinnett	April 1735	41	Ann Bourne	3	May 19, 1777	42
George Walton	1740s	Twenties or thirties	Dorothy Camber	At least 2	February 2, 1804	Fifties or sixties

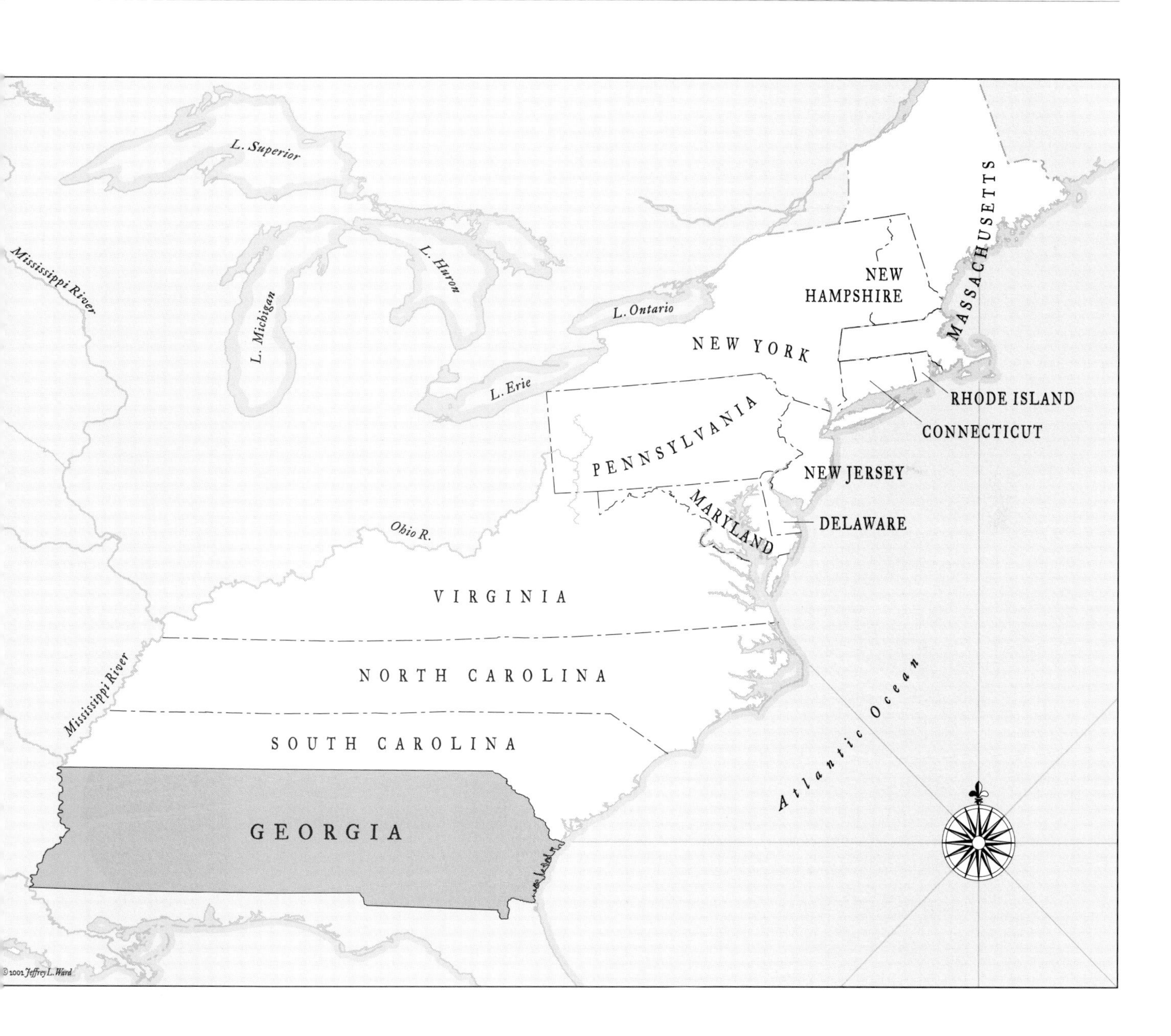

LYMAN HALL:

The Lone Georgian

Lyman Hall

WITH THE HIGHEST PERCENTAGE of Loyalists, Georgia was the only colony that sent no delegates to the First Continental Congress. And for a while, Lyman Hall was the only Georgian at the Second Continental Congress.

Hall lived his first thirty-two years in Connecticut. Born there in 1724, he graduated from Connecticut's Yale College. For a few years, everything went wrong for him. He became a minister, but quarreled with his congregation and was fired. He married Abigail Burr, but she died a year later.

For a new career, Hall chose medicine. Like many other doctors of the 1700s, his medical training consisted of working as an apprentice for an established physician for a time. He also married again, and with his second wife, Mary Osborne Hall, he had one child, a son.

The Halls decided that there was more opportunity for a young doctor in the South. They moved to South Carolina, then continued farther south to Georgia. In the region of the Midway Settlement, near Savannah, Dr. Hall practiced medicine and operated a rice plantation. This area was home to many people from New England who tended to be more anti-English than other Georgians. Hall became a leader of the region's rebels and made rousing speeches supporting the patriot cause.

When Georgia sent no delegates to the First Continental Congress and did the same at the start of the Second Congress, people around Midway were angry. They more or less withdrew from the Georgia Colony and sent Lyman Hall to represent them at the Second Congress in the spring of 1775. Dr. Hall took a seat as a representative of just the Midway area rather than as an official Georgia delegate. Still, his presence in Philadelphia showed that some Georgians were ready to join with the other colonies.

Over the next few weeks, the war intensified and Georgia's leaders realized they must act. In July 1775 Georgia named a delegation, including Lyman Hall, to officially represent the colony in Congress. A year later Hall was one of the three Georgia delegates to sign the Declaration of Independence.

The British invaded Georgia in 1778 and, among other things, destroyed the Halls' home and rice plantation. Dr. Hall escaped with his family to Connecticut, where he remained until the end of the war. He then returned to Georgia and served for a year as the new state's governor. Governor Lyman Hall helped begin the school that became the University of Georgia—one of the nation's first state-supported colleges.

In 1790 the ex-governor invested his savings in a plantation near Augusta. Dr. Lyman Hall, who had once been the lone Georgian in Congress, died at his new plantation a few months later in October of 1790 at the age of sixty-six.

BUTTON GWINNETT:
His Temper Got the Best of Him

Button Gwinnett

THE SIGNER WITH THE ODDEST NAME was born in England in 1735. His first name, Button, was in honor of his godmother, Barbara Button. His last name is pronounced *Gwin-NETT*, with the accent on the second syllable.

When he was in his early twenties, Button Gwinnett married Ann Bourne and went into business as a merchant. He enjoyed speaking with the sailors who carried his goods to the thirteen colonies. Gwinnett was so intrigued by their descriptions of America that in 1764 he and Ann moved to the new country, soon settling in Savannah, Georgia.

Button Gwinnett opened a general store in Savannah, but he didn't do well as a storekeeper. The Gwinnetts, who had three children, decided to try farming instead. They bought St. Catherines Island, off the Georgia coast, and set up a plantation. Unfortunately, Gwinnett didn't do well as a farmer, either.

In 1769 Gwinnett was elected to Georgia's colonial legislature. Although he loved America, he had lived most of his life in England, and he was undecided about which side to take until 1775. It was said that Dr. Lyman Hall convinced him to support his adopted country.

Button Gwinnett was elected to the Second Continental Congress in early 1776. He served for just a few months in Congress, but they were crucial months. Gwinnett voted for and signed the Declaration, then returned to Georgia. He was elected speaker of the Georgia legislature, where he helped frame the state constitution in early 1777. He also served briefly as Georgia's governor. But what he wanted to do most was lead Georgia's troops in battle. Instead, General Lachlan McIntosh, a seasoned soldier, was placed in charge of Georgia's troops.

Jealous and angry, Gwinnett feuded with McIntosh. In the spring of 1777 Governor Gwinnett sent an expedition to seize British-held Florida, limiting General McIntosh's role in the attack. The mission failed. Many people blamed

Gwinnett, who was defeated in the election for governor on May 8, 1777. But when both men appeared before the legislature to explain the failed attack, Gwinnett outtalked McIntosh, and the Georgia lawmakers sided with Gwinnett. McIntosh, enraged at being blamed for the unsuccessful attack, called Gwinnett "a scoundrel and a lying rascal" in front of the Georgia lawmakers.

Gwinnett challenged McIntosh to a pistol duel over the insult. The two men met on the outskirts of Savannah on the morning of May 16 and at a signal fired their guns from a distance of only twelve feet apart. Each man shot the other. McIntosh recovered, but Button Gwinnett died three days later, on May 19, 1777. He was the second signer to die, following John Morton of Pennsylvania by seven weeks.

The Gwinnett family's sufferings weren't over. The British seized his St. Catherines Island estate during the war. It appears that his wife and daughter died before the war ended.

Because Gwinnett's public career was brief, his signature is rare and valuable. A document autographed by the Georgia signer whose temper got the best of him has sold for as much as $100,000.

GEORGE WALTON:
Shot in Battle

Geo Walton.

As is true of many of the signers, we know much more about George Walton's later years than about his early life.

By various accounts he was born in 1740, 1741, or 1749. His birthplace was Virginia, but exactly where is not certain either. George's parents died when he was a child. He was taken in by his aunt and uncle, who apprenticed him to a carpenter when he was about fifteen. It was said that George saved the wood chips from his master's carpentry shop. Then at night he burned them and, by their light, taught himself to read.

Around the age of twenty-two George finished his apprenticeship, but he did not become a carpenter. Instead he moved to Savannah, Georgia, where he studied law. He became an attorney in 1774, and the next year he married Dorothy Camber, with whom he had at least two children.

Walton quickly became one of Georgia's leading lawyers. Like Lyman Hall, he made impassioned speeches against British injustice. He took part in the drive to seize power from Georgia's British rulers, and in 1776 he was selected as one of his colony's delegates to the Continental Congress. Walton took his seat in Congress on July 1 and voted for independence the next day.

In late 1777 George Walton left Congress with the intention of serving as a soldier. He was made a colonel in the Georgia militia and in December 1778 fought the British at Savannah. During the battle, Walton was shot in the thigh by an enemy bullet and knocked off his horse. He was captured and imprisoned. Finally, in the fall of 1779, the Americans and British did a prisoner exchange, and George Walton was released.

Soon after he was freed, Walton was elected governor of Georgia. Later he was elected chief justice of the state and also served in the U.S. Senate. The Georgia signer who had been wounded fighting for independence died in 1804, at the age of anywhere from fifty-five to sixty-four.

XIII. NEW YORK

Henry Hudson, an explorer for the Netherlands, arrived in what is now New York in 1609. The Dutch claimed a large piece of America as New Netherland, of which the New York section was the biggest and most important part. In 1624 the Dutch founded Fort Orange, New York's first colonial town. The next year they began laying out New Amsterdam, which would become the United States's largest city.

In 1664 English warships forced the Dutch to give up New Netherland. The English gave new names to places in the former Dutch colony. The main part of New Netherland they called New York, for James, the English duke of York and Albany. Fort Orange became Albany, and New Amsterdam became New York City.

New York today is one of the most populous of the fifty states. But colonial New York was just average in population. By 1775 it had 190,000 people—roughly the same as Connecticut. New York City, today the nation's largest city, had 25,000 people in 1775 and ranked second to Philadelphia.

During the Revolution, New York was the colony with the most Loyalists. This was because it was home to many wealthy merchants and landowners who didn't want anything to change. Not until July 9, 1776, did New York lawmakers who had gathered in White Plains, New York, approve the Declaration. Lewis Morris, Philip Livingston, Francis Lewis, and William Floyd signed the document for New York. Despite all its Loyalists, New York had thousands of people who fought for independence. Nearly 100 of the war's approximately 300 battles took place in what became known as the Empire State.

NEW YORK

ame	Birth Date	Age at Signing	Marriage(s)	Children	Death Date	Age at Death
EWIS MORRIS	April 8, 1726	50	Mary Walton	10	January 22, 1798	71
HILIP LIVINGSTON	January 15, 1716	60	Christina Ten Broeck	9	June 12, 1778	62
RANCIS LEWIS	March 21, 1713	63	Elizabeth Annesley	7	December 31, 1802	89
ILLIAM FLOYD	December 17, 1734	41	Hannah Jones Joanna Strong	3	August 4, 1821	86

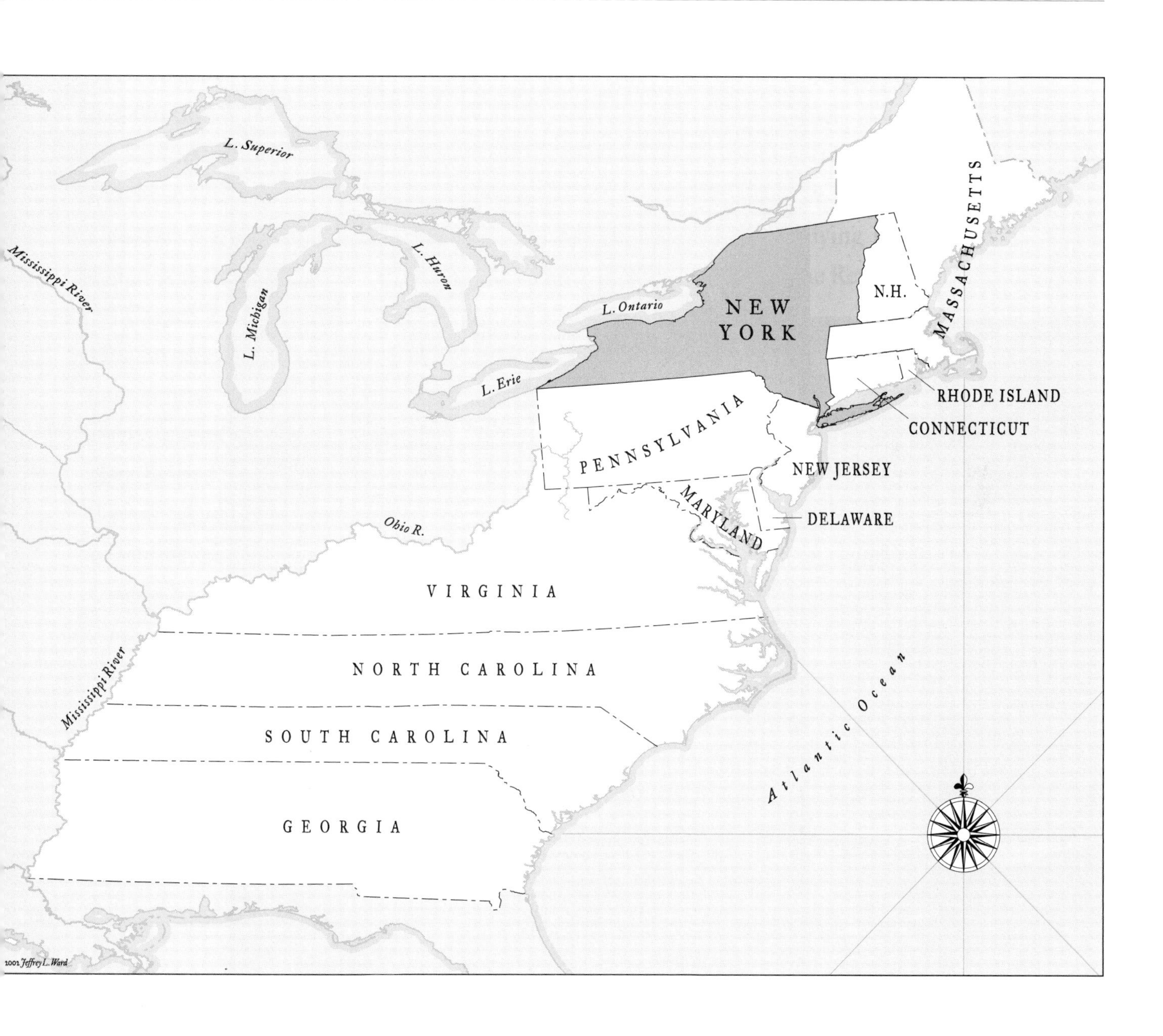

LEWIS MORRIS:
Unlikely Rebel

Lewis Morris

IN GENERAL, the most rebellious colonists were poorer people who hoped that independence would improve their lives. Satisfied with what they had, well-to-do people tended to be Loyalists. Many of the signers were rich men who were exceptions to this rule. One of the unlikeliest rebels was a wealthy New Yorker, Lewis Morris.

Morris was born in what is now New York City in 1726. His family's estate, Morrisania, covered about 2,000 acres, or roughly three square miles, and resembled a small town, with farmers who rented land, blacksmiths, carpenters, and slaves. Lewis attended Yale College, but left without earning a degree. As his family's oldest son, he was expected to devote his time and energy into learning to run Morrisania, which would one day be his.

For many years Morris followed the typical pattern of a wealthy gentleman. At twenty-three he married rich young Mary Walton, with whom he had six sons and four daughters. Upon his father's death in 1762, Lewis Morris became the lord of Morrisania Manor.

Following in the footsteps of his grandfather, who had been the royal governor of New Jersey, and of his father, who had been a judge, Lewis decided to enter public service. He was elected to the New York legislature in 1769. As a prosperous landowner, Lewis Morris seemed likely to remain loyal to England, but he surprised people by taking America's side. In fact, while other colonies were sending their leading rebels to the First Continental Congress in 1774, Morris was *not* chosen because he opposed the Mother Country so firmly.

New York gradually caught up to Morris's way of thinking, and he was sent to the Second Continental Congress in May 1775. He served on the committee assigned to supply the troops with weapons and ammunition. On July 2, 1776, when every colony but New York voted for independence, Morris was back home.

He attended New York's convention in White Plains that approved the Declaration on July 9, then returned to Philadelphia and signed the document.

During the war the British burned and wrecked Morrisania. Lewis Morris spent many years rebuilding his estate. Between 1777 and 1790 he also served on and off in the New York State Senate.

Lewis Morris's brother Gouverneur Morris wrote much of the final draft of the U.S. Constitution. Lewis attended the convention held in Poughkeepsie, New York, to determine whether New York would accept the Constitution. Thanks partly to his efforts, New York approved the Constitution on July 26, 1788, by a razor-thin vote of 30 in favor to 27 opposed. With that vote, New York became our eleventh state. Lewis Morris, the unlikely rebel, died at Morrisania in 1798 at the age of seventy-one.

PHILIP LIVINGSTON:
Reluctant Rebel

Phil. Livingston

PHILIP LIVINGSTON IS REMEMBERED for signing the Declaration of Independence and helping to win the Revolution. He might find that ironic, for just the words *independence* and *revolution* were enough to make him shudder.

Livingston was born into an extremely prosperous family in Albany, New York, in 1716. Livingston Manor, his family's estate, covered 160,000 acres—250 square miles, about a fifth the size of Rhode Island! Young Philip was tutored at home, then sent to Yale College, graduating in 1737. Three years later he married Christina Ten Broeck, daughter of the mayor of Albany. The couple, who would have nine children, maintained two lovely homes in what is now New York City.

Livingston was a very successful merchant who imported British goods and sold them in America. He devoted much of his time and money to civic improvements, helping to begin the New York Chamber of Commerce, the New York Hospital, and the New York Society Library. In addition, he helped establish what are now Columbia University in New York City and Rutgers University in New Jersey.

He also entered politics. In 1758 Livingston was elected to New York's colonial legislature. As the trouble with England developed, he favored moderation. Livingston despised the British taxes, saying that "being taxed only with our own consent" was the "great badge of English liberty." Yet he opposed the violent acts of the Sons of Liberty and dreaded the prospect of war. Independence was "the most vain, empty, shallow, and ridiculous project," he warned, and predicted that America would quickly collapse if it separated from England.

In 1774 Livingston was sent to the Continental Congress, where he served for the last four years of his life. He eventually accepted the fact that independence was coming and did everything he could to help his country. Livingston signed the Declaration in August 1776 and served on a number of congressional committees, including the Secret Committee, which imported weapons and gunpowder for the army. He spent a great deal of his own money in obtaining these military supplies.

For Philip Livingston, the Revolution meant personal ruin. His family had to flee to Kingston, New York, and the British seized his two New York City homes, turning one into a military hospital and the other into a barracks for enemy troops. Livingston didn't live to see the winning of independence. At a point when victory was still far off, sixty-two-year-old Philip Livingston died while attending Congress in 1778.

FRANCIS LEWIS:
He Lost Nearly Everything

Few signers lost as much as Francis Lewis in the Revolution, yet how many people today even know who he was?

He was born in Wales, a country next to England that is part of Great Britain, in 1713. Both his parents died when he was very young. Francis grew up with relatives in Wales and Scotland, then went to school in London. As a young man, he worked in a London countinghouse.

In his twenties Francis Lewis became a merchant and moved to America, settling in New York City. He married Elizabeth Annesley, his partner's sister, in 1745. Lewis and Elizabeth had seven children, but only three of them survived infancy.

Francis Lewis shipped goods to many parts of the world, often going along to sell the cargo. He was believed to be the first American businessman to visit Russia. He also sailed to Africa, to various European ports, and to Scotland's Orkney Islands. Twice he was shipwrecked off Ireland's coast. He even voyaged through the Arctic Ocean in the world's far northern regions.

Back in America, Lewis helped Britain fight France in the French and Indian War (1754–63), serving as a military aide at Fort Oswego in New York. When the French attacked the fort in 1756, several British officers standing near Lewis were killed. He was captured, and given to the Frenchmen's Indian friends as a prisoner. Lewis reportedly convinced the Indians to spare his life by somehow communicating with them in the Welsh language. He was later sent to France, where he was held until the war ended in 1763. Finally, after seven years as a prisoner, he returned home. The British rewarded him for his war service by granting him 5,000 acres (about eight square miles) of land. In 1765 he retired from business and moved from New York City to Long Island, New York.

That same year, England passed the Stamp Act. Enraged by this and other

British taxes, Francis Lewis joined protest groups. In April 1775 he was elected to the Continental Congress, where he worked to build the navy and to supply the army with weapons. He performed his most famous deed when he signed the Declaration of Independence on August 2, 1776.

In the autumn of 1776, the British, who had seized New York City, approached Francis Lewis's Long Island home. They destroyed it and took his wife prisoner. Elizabeth Lewis was held in a cold, filthy prison in New York City for several months to strike back at her husband for signing the Declaration. The experience ruined Elizabeth Lewis's health, and she died about two years later. To make things worse, Francis Lewis was estranged from his only daughter, who married a British navy officer and settled in England.

Francis Lewis, who had lost his wife, his daughter, and his home, retired from Congress in 1781 and lived with his two sons for the rest of his life. He died on New Year's Eve of 1802 at the age of eighty-nine.

WILLIAM FLOYD:
His Home Became a Stable

BECAUSE NEW YORK WAS ONE of the main battlegrounds of the Revolution, its patriots, including the William Floyd family, faced great danger during the war.

William Floyd was born into a wealthy family on Long Island in 1734. He had little schooling. Instead, he was trained to run the family estate, which he had to do starting at age eighteen when his father died. In his mid-twenties William married Hannah Jones, with whom he had three children. Floyd was said to be a simple man whose greatest pleasures were hunting and hosting parties for his friends.

In 1769 Floyd became an official of Brookhaven, the Long Island town where his estate stood. But his political interests remained local until the troubles with England heated up in the 1770s. Because he spoke strongly against British taxes, he was elected to the Continental Congress in 1774. Unlike most of the other congressmen, Floyd was neither a lawyer nor an experienced politician. He earned his colleagues' respect by his work on the naval board and other committees, and by quietly listening to the debates. He signed the Declaration of Independence on August 2, 1776.

Besides serving in Congress, Floyd led a New York militia unit. In one skirmish, he and his troops drove off British invaders who were trying to land on Long Island. But the British defeated the Americans on Long Island shortly after Floyd signed the Declaration. Fortunately Hannah was warned of the British approach before the enemy seized the Floyd estate. She and her children fled and were rowed across Long Island Sound to Connecticut by some fishermen. For the rest of the war, William Floyd's family hid in Middletown, Connecticut. Hannah Floyd died in 1781—perhaps partly as a result of the hardships of war.

Peace was made in 1783, and William Floyd returned home after about eight years of service in Congress. He found that a party of British cavalry (horse soldiers) had used his home as their barracks and had wrecked the place. Floyd rebuilt his estate, and the next year he married Joanna Strong.

William Floyd continued to serve his country. He was elected to the first U.S. House of Representatives, where he held office from 1789 to 1791. Ten years later, in 1801, he was a delegate to the convention that rewrote New York's state constitution.

In his old age, William Floyd became infected with the "pioneer spirit." In 1803, at the age of nearly seventy, he pulled up stakes and moved with his family to a frontier region on New York's Mohawk River. He was elected to represent this frontier district in the state senate in 1808, but by then he was well into his seventies and wasn't able to spend much time in Albany, the capital of the Empire State. William Floyd died on his farm on the New York frontier at the age of eighty-six on August 4, 1821—forty-five years and two days after he had signed the Declaration of Independence.

IN CONGRESS, JULY 4, 1776.

The unanimous Declaration of the thirteen united States of America.

When in the Course of human events, it becomes necessary for one people to dissolve the political bands which have connected them with another, and to assume among the powers of the earth, the separate and equal station to which the Laws of Nature and of Nature's God entitle them, a decent respect to the opinions of mankind requires that they should declare the causes which impel them to the separation. —— We hold these truths to be self-evident, that all men are created equal, that they are endowed by their Creator with certain unalienable Rights, that among these are Life, Liberty and the pursuit of Happiness. — That to secure these rights, Governments are instituted among Men, deriving their just powers from the consent of the governed, — That whenever any Form of Government becomes destructive of these ends, it is the Right of the People to alter or to abolish it, and to institute new Government, laying its foundation on such principles and organizing its powers in such form, as to them shall seem most likely to effect their Safety and Happiness. Prudence, indeed, will dictate that Governments long established should not be changed for light and transient causes; and accordingly all experience hath shewn, that mankind are more disposed to suffer, while evils are sufferable, than to right themselves by abolishing the forms to which they are accustomed. But when a long train of abuses and usurpations, pursuing invariably the same Object evinces a design to reduce them under absolute Despotism, it is their right, it is their duty, to throw off such Government, and to provide new Guards for their future security. — Such has been the patient sufferance of these Colonies; and such is now the necessity which constrains them to alter their former Systems of Government. The history of the present King of Great Britain is a history of repeated injuries and usurpations, all having in direct object the establishment of an absolute Tyranny over these States. To prove this, let Facts be submitted to a candid world. —— He has refused his Assent to Laws, the most wholesome and necessary for the public good. —— He has forbidden his Governors to pass Laws of immediate and pressing importance, unless suspended in their operation till his Assent should be obtained; and when so suspended, he has utterly neglected to attend to them. —— He has refused to pass other Laws for the accommodation of large districts of people, unless those people would relinquish the right of Representation in the Legislature, a right inestimable to them and formidable to tyrants only. —— He has called together legislative bodies at places unusual, uncomfortable, and distant from the depository of their Public Records, for the sole purpose of fatiguing them into compliance with his measures. —— He has dissolved Representative Houses repeatedly, for opposing with manly firmness his invasions on the rights of the people. —— He has refused for a long time, after such dissolutions, to cause others to be elected; whereby the Legislative powers, incapable of Annihilation, have returned to the People at large for their exercise; the State remaining in the mean time exposed to all the dangers of invasion from without, and convulsions within. —— He has endeavoured to prevent the population of these States; for that purpose obstructing the Laws for Naturalization of Foreigners; refusing to pass others to encourage their migrations hither, and raising the conditions of new Appropriations of Lands. —— He has obstructed the Administration of Justice, by refusing his Assent to Laws for establishing Judiciary powers. —— He has made Judges dependent on his Will alone, for the tenure of their offices, and the amount and payment of their salaries. —— He has erected a multitude of New Offices, and sent hither swarms of Officers to harrass our people, and eat out their substance. —— He has kept among us, in times of peace, Standing Armies without the Consent of our legislatures. —— He has affected to render the Military independent of and superior to the Civil power. —— He has combined with others to subject us to a jurisdiction foreign to our constitution, and unacknowledged by our laws; giving his Assent to their Acts of pretended Legislation: — For Quartering large bodies of armed troops among us: — For protecting them, by a mock Trial, from punishment for any Murders which they should commit on the Inhabitants of these States: — For cutting off our Trade with all parts of the world: — For imposing Taxes on us without our Consent: — For depriving us in many cases, of the benefits of Trial by Jury: — For transporting us beyond Seas to be tried for pretended offences: — For abolishing the free System of English Laws in a neighbouring Province, establishing therein an Arbitrary government, and enlarging its Boundaries so as to render it at once an example and fit instrument for introducing the same absolute rule into these Colonies: — For taking away our Charters, abolishing our most valuable Laws, and altering fundamentally the Forms of our Governments: — For suspending our own Legislatures, and declaring themselves invested with power to legislate for us in all cases whatsoever. — He has abdicated Government here, by declaring us out of his Protection and waging War against us. —— He has plundered our seas, ravaged our Coasts, burnt our towns, and destroyed the lives of our people. —— He is at this time transporting large Armies of foreign Mercenaries to compleat the works of death, desolation and tyranny, already begun with circumstances of Cruelty & perfidy scarcely paralleled in the most barbarous ages, and totally unworthy the Head of a civilized nation. —— He has constrained our fellow Citizens taken Captive on the high Seas to bear Arms against their Country, to become the executioners of their friends and Brethren, or to fall themselves by their Hands. —— He has excited domestic insurrections amongst us, and has endeavoured to bring on the inhabitants of our frontiers, the merciless Indian Savages, whose known rule of warfare, is an undistinguished destruction of all ages, sexes and conditions. In every stage of these Oppressions We have Petitioned for Redress in the most humble terms: Our repeated Petitions have been answered only by repeated injury. A Prince, whose character is thus marked by every act which may define a Tyrant, is unfit to be the ruler of a free people. Nor have We been wanting in attentions to our Brittish brethren. We have warned them from time to time of attempts by their legislature to extend an unwarrantable jurisdiction over us. We have reminded them of the circumstances of our emigration and settlement here. We have appealed to their native justice and magnanimity, and we have conjured them by the ties of our common kindred to disavow these usurpations, which, would inevitably interrupt our connections and correspondence. They too have been deaf to the voice of justice and of consanguinity. We must, therefore, acquiesce in the necessity, which denounces our Separation, and hold them, as we hold the rest of mankind, Enemies in War, in Peace Friends. ——

We, therefore, the Representatives of the united States of America, in General Congress, Assembled, appealing to the Supreme Judge of the world for the rectitude of our intentions, do, in the Name, and by Authority of the good People of these Colonies, solemnly publish and declare, That these United Colonies are, and of Right ought to be Free and Independent States; that they are Absolved from all Allegiance to the British Crown, and that all political connection between them and the State of Great Britain, is and ought to be totally dissolved; and that as Free and Independent States, they have full Power to levy War, conclude Peace, contract Alliances, establish Commerce, and to do all other Acts and Things which Independent States may of right do. —— And for the support of this Declaration, with a firm reliance on the protection of divine Providence, we mutually pledge to each other our Lives, our Fortunes and our sacred Honor.

John Hancock

Button Gwinnett
Lyman Hall
Geo Walton.

Wm Hooper
Joseph Hewes,
John Penn
Edward Rutledge.
Thos Heyward Junr.
Thomas Lynch Junr.
Arthur Middleton

Samuel Chase
Wm Paca
Thos Stone
Charles Carroll of Carrollton
George Wythe
Richard Henry Lee
Th Jefferson
Benja Harrison
Thos Nelson jr.
Francis Lightfoot Lee
Carter Braxton

Robt Morris
Benjamin Rush
Benja Franklin
John Morton
Geo Clymer
Jas Smith
Geo. Taylor
James Wilson
Geo. Ross
Caesar Rodney
Geo Read
Tho M:Kean

Wm Floyd
Phil. Livingston
Frans Lewis
Lewis Morris
Richd Stockton
Jno Witherspoon
Fras Hopkinson
John Hart
Abra Clark

Josiah Bartlett
Wm Whipple
Saml Adams
John Adams
Robt Treat Paine
Elbridge Gerry
Step Hopkins
William Ellery
Roger Sherman
Saml Huntington
Wm Williams
Oliver Wolcott
Matthew Thornton

The Declaration of Independence

IN CONGRESS, July 4, 1776.

The unanimous Declaration of the thirteen United States of America,

When in the Course of human events, it becomes necessary for one people to dissolve the political bands which have connected them with another, and to assume among the powers of the earth, the separate and equal station to which the Laws of Nature and of Nature's God entitle them, a decent respect to the opinions of mankind requires that they should declare the causes which impel them to the separation.

We hold these truths to be self-evident, that all men are created equal, that they are endowed by their Creator with certain unalienable Rights, that among these are Life, Liberty and the pursuit of Happiness.—That to secure these rights, Governments are instituted among Men, deriving their just powers from the consent of the governed,—That whenever any Form of Government becomes destructive of these ends, it is the Right of the People to alter or to abolish it, and to institute new Government, laying its foundation on such principles and organizing its powers in such form, as to them shall seem most likely to effect their Safety and Happiness. Prudence, indeed, will dictate that Governments long established should not be changed for light and transient causes; and accordingly all experience hath shewn, that mankind are more disposed to suffer, while evils are sufferable, than to right themselves by abolishing the forms to which they are accustomed. But when a long train of abuses and usurpations, pursuing invariably the same Object evinces a design to reduce them under absolute Despotism, it is their right, it is their duty, to throw off such Government, and to provide new Guards for their future security.—Such has been the patient sufferance of these Colonies; and such is now the necessity which constrains them to alter their former Systems of Government. The history of the present King of Great Britain is a history of repeated injuries and usurpations, all having in direct object the establishment of an absolute Tyranny over these States. To prove this, let Facts be submitted to a candid world.

He has refused his Assent to Laws, the most wholesome and necessary for the public good.

He has forbidden his Governors to pass Laws of immediate and pressing importance, unless suspended in their operation till his Assent should be obtained; and when so suspended, he has utterly neglected to attend to them.

He has refused to pass other Laws for the accommodation of large districts of people, unless those people would relinquish the right of Representation in the Legislature, a right inestimable to them and formidable to tyrants only.

He has called together legislative bodies at places unusual, uncomfortable, and distant from the depository of their public Records, for the sole purpose of fatiguing them into compliance with his measures.

He has dissolved Representative Houses repeatedly, for opposing with manly firmness his invasions on the rights of the people.

He has refused for a long time, after such dissolutions, to cause others to be elected; whereby the Legislative powers, incapable of Annihilation, have returned to the People at large for their exercise; the State remaining in the mean time exposed to all the dangers of invasion from without, and convulsions within.

He has endeavoured to prevent the population of these States; for that purpose obstructing the Laws for Naturalization of Foreigners; refusing to pass others to encourage their migrations hither, and raising the conditions of new Appropriations of Lands.

He has obstructed the Administration of Justice, by refusing his Assent to Laws for establishing Judiciary powers.

He has made Judges dependent on his Will alone, for the tenure of their offices, and the amount and payment of their salaries.

He has erected a multitude of New Offices, and sent hither swarms of Officers to harass our people, and eat out their substance.

He has kept among us, in times of peace, Standing Armies without the Consent of our legislatures.

He has affected to render the Military independent of and superior to the Civil power.

He has combined with others to subject us to a jurisdiction foreign to our constitution, and unacknowledged by our laws; giving his Assent to their Acts of pretended Legislation:

For quartering large bodies of armed troops among us:

For protecting them, by a mock Trial, from punishment for any Murders which they should commit on the Inhabitants of these States:

For cutting off our Trade with all parts of the world:

For imposing Taxes on us without our Consent:

For depriving us in many cases, of the benefits of Trial by Jury:

For transporting us beyond Seas to be tried for pretended offences:

For abolishing the free System of English Laws in a neighbouring Province, establishing therein an Arbitrary government, and enlarging its Boundaries so as to render it at once an example and fit instrument for introducing the same absolute rule into these Colonies:

For taking away our Charters, abolishing our most valuable Laws, and altering fundamentally the Forms of our Governments: For suspending our own Legislatures, and declaring themselves invested with power to legislate for us in all cases whatsoever.

He has abdicated Government here, by declaring us out of his Protection and waging War against us.

He has plundered our seas, ravaged our Coasts, burnt our towns, and destroyed the lives of our people.

He is at this time transporting large Armies of foreign Mercenaries to compleat the works of death, desolation and tyranny, already begun with circumstances of Cruelty & perfidy scarcely paralleled in the most barbarous ages, and totally unworthy the Head of a civilized nation.

He has constrained our fellow Citizens taken Captive on the high Seas to bear Arms against their Country, to become the executioners of their friends and Brethren, or to fall themselves by their Hands.

He has excited domestic insurrections amongst us, and has endeavoured to bring on the inhabitants of our frontiers, the merciless Indian Savages, whose known rule of warfare, is an undistinguished destruction of all ages, sexes and conditions.

In every stage of these Oppressions We have Petitioned for Redress in the most humble terms: Our repeated Petitions have been answered only by repeated injury. A Prince whose character is thus marked by every act which may define a Tyrant, is unfit to be the ruler of a free people. Nor have We been wanting in attentions to our British brethren. We have warned them from time to time of attempts by their legislature to extend an unwarrantable jurisdiction over us. We have reminded them of the circumstances of our emigration and settlement here. We have appealed to their native justice and magnanimity, and we have conjured them by the ties of our common kindred to disavow these usurpations, which, would inevitably interrupt our connections and correspondence. They too have been deaf to the voice of justice and of consanguinity. We must, therefore, acquiesce in the necessity, which denounces our Separation, and hold them, as we hold the rest of mankind, Enemies in War, in Peace Friends.—

We, therefore, the Representatives of the United States of America, in General Congress, Assembled, appealing to the Supreme Judge of the world for the rectitude of our intentions, do, in the Name, and by Authority of the good People of these Colonies, solemnly publish and declare, That these United Colonies are, and of Right ought to be Free and Independent States; that they are Absolved from all Allegiance to the British Crown, and that all political connection between them and the State of Great Britain, is and ought to be totally dissolved; and that as Free and Independent States, they have full Power to levy War, conclude Peace, contract Alliances, establish Commerce, and to do all other Acts and Things which Independent States may of right do.—And for the support of this Declaration, with a firm reliance on the protection of Divine Providence, we mutually pledge to each other our Lives, our Fortunes and our sacred Honor.

The 56 signatures on the Declaration appear in the positions indicated:

[*Column* 1]

GEORGIA:
- Button Gwinnett
- Lyman Hall
- George Walton

[*Column* 2]

NORTH CAROLINA:
- William Hooper
- Joseph Hewes
- John Penn

SOUTH CAROLINA:
- Edward Rutledge
- Thomas Heyward Jr.
- Thomas Lynch Jr.
- Arthur Middleton

[*Column* 3]

MASSACHUSETTS:
- John Hancock

MARYLAND:
- Samuel Chase
- William Paca
- Thomas Stone
- Charles Carroll of Carrollton

VIRGINIA:
- George Wythe
- Richard Henry Lee
- Thomas Jefferson
- Benjamin Harrison
- Thomas Nelson Jr.
- Francis Lightfoot Lee
- Carter Braxton

[*Column 4*]

PENNSYLVANIA:

Robert Morris
Benjamin Rush
Benjamin Franklin
John Morton
George Clymer
James Smith
George Taylor
James Wilson
George Ross

DELAWARE:

Caesar Rodney
George Read
Thomas McKean

[*Column 5*]

NEW YORK:

William Floyd
Philip Livingston
Francis Lewis
Lewis Morris

NEW JERSEY:

Richard Stockton
John Witherspoon
Francis Hopkinson
John Hart
Abraham Clark

[*Column 6*]

NEW HAMPSHIRE:

Josiah Bartlett
William Whipple

MASSACHUSETTS:

Samuel Adams
John Adams
Robert Treat Paine
Elbridge Gerry

RHODE ISLAND:

Stephen Hopkins
William Ellery

CONNECTICUT:

Roger Sherman
Samuel Huntington
William Williams
Oliver Wolcott

NEW HAMPSHIRE:

Matthew Thornton

Afterword

For several years after independence was declared, it appeared that America would lose its struggle for liberty and that the signers might end up "hanging together" on the British gallows. George Washington's army at its peak contained 20,000 men, compared to 50,000 for the enemy forces. Congress couldn't afford to arm, clothe, or pay its troops properly. At times, American soldiers had to pick berries and shoot squirrels to keep from starving. A few days before Christmas of 1777, Washington marched his 11,000 men into winter quarters at Valley Forge, Pennsylvania. Entering their winter camp, the men left a bloody trail on the frozen ground, for half of them no longer had shoes. More than 3,000 troops—over a quarter of the army—died of cold, hunger, and disease during that terrible winter at Valley Forge.

But eventually the tide turned. Thanks mostly to Benjamin Franklin's efforts, France joined America's side in the spring of 1778. French money, soldiers, sailors, ships, and weapons were a great boost to the Americans, who also had two other advantages: They were fighting on their home soil, and they had a core of patriots who would never give up. General Washington awaited his chance to deal the British a crushing blow. It finally came in October 1781, when, with French help, the Americans defeated a huge British army at Yorktown, Virginia, ending major Revolutionary War fighting. On September 3, 1783, the final peace treaty was signed. Britain now recognized the United States as a free and independent nation.

Even while the Revolution was not yet won, Americans began celebrating July 4 as Independence Day. Down to the present time, John Adams's expectation for how July 2 would be "solemnized" has held true for July 4. Americans celebrate the day "with pomp and parade, with shows, games, sports, bells, bonfires, from one end of this continent to the other," just as Adams predicted. He omitted fireworks and picnics, but he couldn't have foreseen everything when he wrote these words to his wife Abigail on July 3, 1776!

Of course the Declaration means more to Americans than a day for parades and fireworks. To many Americans, the Declaration is the most beloved government document, and its best-known passage perfectly expresses what the country stands for: "We hold these truths to be self-evident, that all men are created equal, that they are endowed by their Creator with certain unalienable Rights, that among these are Life, Liberty, and the pursuit of Happiness."

Each generation of Americans has been called upon to defend the ideas embodied in the Declaration in one way or another. About thirty years after the Revolution ended, the country had to fight off the British again in the War of 1812 to maintain its status as a sovereign nation. A few years after that, the country began arguing bitterly about slavery. Opponents of the evil institution pointed out that the paper that created the United States declared that *all* people were created equal and entitled to their liberty. How could the country boast of its Declaration of Independence and yet hold black people in bondage? From 1861 to 1865 the country fought the Civil War mainly over slavery. This conflict cost more American lives than any other war in history, but it freed the country's four million slaves.

How could the nation assert that everyone has "certain unalienable Rights" and yet not allow half its citizens to vote? In the late 1800s and early 1900s, thousands of fair-minded Americans fought for women's right to vote, which was finally achieved in 1920.

There are people still living who remember the two deadliest wars human beings have ever waged. Called World War I (1914–18) and World War II (1939–45), they both involved numerous countries. Had the United States not helped win these conflicts, the lives and liberties of many millions of the world's people would have been lost.

In the 1950s and 1960s, the civil rights of black people became a leading issue. Dr. Martin Luther King Jr. quoted the Declaration of Independence in his famous "I Have a Dream" speech during the March on Washington in 1963. "I have a dream that one day this nation will rise up and live out the true meaning of its creed," said Dr. King. "*We hold these truths to be self-evident, that all men are created equal.*" This phrase is still—and undoubtedly always will be—a motto of groups seeking justice.

Like Americans of the past, a new generation is being asked to defend the Declaration's philosophy. And once again the lives and freedom of countless people are at stake. This time the threat is from international terrorism, which forced the country to go to war once more in 2001.

While speaking in Independence Hall on George Washington's birthday in 1861, Abraham Lincoln revealed what the nation's "birth certificate" meant to him. "I have never had a feeling politically that did not spring from the sentiments embodied in the Declaration of Independence," said the recently elected president. "I have often inquired of myself what great principle or idea it was that kept this [nation] so long together. It was not the mere matter of the separation of the Colonies from the Motherland, but that sentiment in the Declaration of Independence which gave liberty, not alone to the people of this country, but, I hope, to the world, for all future time."

Our sixteenth president was right about the Declaration spreading liberty "to the world." The great document, and the revolution that spawned it, inspired dozens of other revolts against colonial rule in Mexico, Canada, and many countries in Asia, Africa, South and Central America, and other lands. To some degree, billions of people around the world owe their freedom to the ideas behind America's Declaration of Independence.

John Adams may have best expressed the American people's devotion to the Declaration's principles. As July 4, 1826, approached, one of the town's leading men visited Adams's home in Quincy, Massachusetts. The visitor asked the ailing former president to offer a toast that could be used at the local Fourth of July celebration.

"I will give you a toast," ninety-year-old John Adams answered. "I give you: Independence forever!" The visitor asked Adams if he had anything to add. "Not a word," he replied.

A few days later, John Adams lay dying. At a moment when he was conscious, he was asked if he knew what day it was. "Oh, yes, it is the glorious Fourth of July," he replied. "God bless it."

Later that day, John Adams took his last breath. Meanwhile, in another part of Quincy, people were cheering the simple but timeless toast he had left for his fellow Americans:

"Independence forever!"

Illustrator's Note

I was initially worried that I would not be able to find fifty-six visual sources in order to draw my portraits of the signers of the Declaration of Independence. Would I be able to locate suitable pictures of them all? A good number of these men are not familiar to most of us. Some were not at all affluent; and those without wealth presumably would not have been able to afford having their portraits painted. However, the Internet came to my assistance. Those portraits that I could not locate on the World Wide Web, I found in books at the Boston Public Library, with the assistance of John P. Dorsey of that institution and my friend Alison Pierce.

Bibliography

Bakeless, John, and Katherine Bakeless. *Signers of the Declaration.* Boston: Houghton Mifflin, 1969.

Becker, Carl. *The Declaration of Independence: A Study in the History of Political Ideas.* 1922. Reprint, New York: Knopf, 1960.

Billias, George Athan. *Elbridge Gerry.* New York: McGraw-Hill, 1976.

Block, Seymour Stanton. *Benjamin Franklin: His Wit, Wisdom, and Women.* New York: Hastings House, 1975.

Bogin, Ruth. *Abraham Clark and the Quest for Equality in the Revolutionary Era, 1774–1794.* Rutherford, N.J.: Fairleigh Dickinson University Press, 1982.

Booth, Sally Smith. *The Women of '76.* New York: Hastings House, 1973.

Boutell, Lewis Henry. *The Life of Roger Sherman.* Chicago: McClurg, 1896.

Brodie, Fawn M. *Thomas Jefferson: An Intimate History.* New York: Norton, 1974.

Brown, Imogene E. *American Aristides: A Biography of George Wythe.* Rutherford, N.J.: Fairleigh Dickinson University Press, 1981.

Butterfield, L. H., ed. *Diary and Autobiography of John Adams.* 4 vols. Cambridge, Mass.: Harvard University Press, 1961.

Chidsey, Donald Barr. *The World of Samuel Adams.* Nashville, Tenn.: Thomas Nelson, 1974.

Chitwood, Oliver Perry. *Richard Henry Lee: Statesman of the Revolution.* Morgantown: West Virginia University Library, 1967.

Coleman, John M. *Thomas McKean: Forgotten Leader of the Revolution.* Rockaway, N.J.: American Faculty Press, 1975.

Dill, Alonzo Thomas. *Carter Braxton, Virginia Signer.* Lanham, Md.: University Press of America, 1983.

Donovan, Frank. *Mr. Jefferson's Declaration.* New York: Dodd, Mead, 1968.

Elsmere, Jane Shaffer. *Justice Samuel Chase.* Muncie, Ind.: Janevar, 1980.

Evans, Emory G. *Thomas Nelson of Yorktown.* Williamsburg, Va.: Colonial Williamsburg Foundation, 1975.

Fehrenbach, T. R. *Greatness to Spare.* Princeton, N.J.: Van Nostrand, 1968.

Fleming, Thomas. *The Man from Monticello: An Intimate Life of Thomas Jefferson.* New York: Morrow, 1969.

Foster, William E. *Stephen Hopkins: A Rhode Island Statesman.* Providence: Rider, 1884.

Fowler, William M. *The Baron of Beacon Hill: A Biography of John Hancock.* Boston: Houghton Mifflin, 1980.

Fowler, William M. *William Ellery: A Rhode Island Politico and Lord of Admiralty.* Metuchen, N.J.: Scarecrow, 1973.

Friedenwald, Herbert. *The Declaration of Independence: An Interpretation and an Analysis.* New York: Macmillan, 1904.

Garraty, John A., and Mark C. Carnes, eds. *American National Biography.* New York: Oxford University Press, 1999.

Gerlach, Larry R. *Connecticut Congressman: Samuel Huntington, 1731–1796.* Hartford: American Revolution Bicentennial Commission of Connecticut, 1976.

Green, Ashbel. *The Life of the Reverend John Witherspoon.* Reprint. Princeton, N.J.: Princeton University Press, 1973.

Grundfest, Jerry. *George Clymer: Philadelphia Revolutionary, 1739–1813* New York: Arno Press, 1982.

Haw, James. *John and Edward Rutledge of South Carolina.* Athens: University of Georgia Press, 1997.

Hawke, David. *Benjamin Rush: Revolutionary Gadfly.* Indianapolis: Bobbs-Merrill, 1971.

Hawke, David. *A Transaction of Free Men: The Birth and Course of the Declaration of Independence.* New York: Scribner's, 1964.

Hazelton, John H. *The Declaration of Independence: Its History.* New York: Dodd, Mead, 1906.

Lengyel, Cornel Adam. *The Declaration of Independence.* New York: Grosset & Dunlap, 1968.

Malone, Dumas, ed. *Dictionary of American Biography.* New York: Scribner's, 1961.

Malone, Dumas. *The Story of the Declaration of Independence.* New York: Oxford University Press, 1954.

Mevers, Frank C., ed. *The Papers of Josiah Bartlett.* Hanover, N.H.: University Press of New England, 1979.

National Cyclopaedia of American Biography. New York: James T. White & Company, 1894.

Peabody, James Bishop, ed. *John Adams: A Biography in His Own Words.* New York: Newsweek, 1973.

Riley, Stephen T., and Edward W. Hanson, eds. *The Papers of Robert Treat Paine.* 2 vols. Boston: Massachusetts Historical Society, 1992.

Salley, A. S. *Delegates to the Continental Congress from South Carolina, 1774–1789.* Bulletins of the Historical Commission of South Carolina, no. 9. Columbia: Historical Commission of South Carolina, 1927.

Scott, Jane Harrington. *A Gentleman as Well as a Whig: Caesar Rodney and the American Revolution.* Newark: University of Delaware Press, 2000.

Smith, Ellen Hart. *Charles Carroll of Carrollton.* Cambridge, Mass.: Harvard University Press, 1942.

Stark, Bruce P. *Connecticut Signer: William Williams.* Chester, Conn.: Pequot Press, 1975.

Stiverson, Gregory A., and Phebe R. Jacobsen. *William Paca.* Baltimore: Maryland Historical Society, 1976.

Wagner, Frederick. *Patriot's Choice: The Story of John Hancock.* New York: Dodd, Mead, 1964.

Wells, William V. *Life and Public Services of Samuel Adams.* 3 vols. 1866. Reprint, Boston: Little, Brown, 1969.

Wright, Esmond. *Franklin of Philadelphia.* Cambridge, Mass.: Harvard University Press, 1986.

Young, Eleanor. *Forgotten Patriot: Robert Morris.* New York: Macmillan, 1950.

Zall, Paul M., ed. *Comical Spirit of Seventy-Six: The Humor of Francis Hopkinson.* San Marino, Calif.: Huntington Library, 1976.

Index